Persian Painting

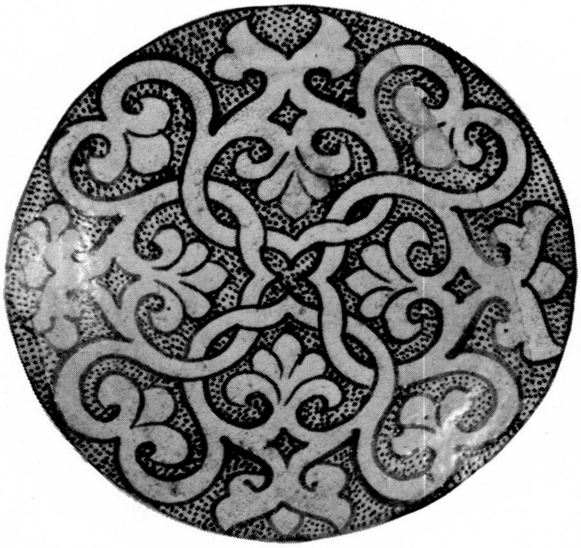

PERSIAN PAINTING

Five Royal Safavid Manuscripts of the Sixteenth Century

STUART CARY WELCH

George Braziller / New York

Published in 1976.

For information address the publisher:

George Braziller, Inc., One Park Avenue, New York, New York 10016

Library of Congress Cataloging in Publication Data

Welch, Stuart Cary.
Persian painting

Bibliography: p.
1. Illumination of books and manuscripts, Iranian.
2. Miniature painting, Iranian. I. Title.
ND3241.W44 745.6′7′0955 75-38508
ISBN 0-8076-0812-2
ISBN 0-8076-8013-0 pbk.

Second Printing

Printed by Mohndruck in West Germany

DESIGNED BY RONALD FARBER

Frontispiece: Detail of ceramic plate from excavation at Nishapur, India. The Metropolitan Museum of Art, Museum Excavations, 1939, Rogers Fund.

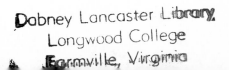

Acknowledgments

Most of all, I am grateful to Martin Bernard Dickson, who looked hard at the pictures, for sharing with me his extraordinary knowledge of all aspects of Safavid life. This pleasurable book is dedicated to him. I hope that I have not used his information inaccurately or too loosely. I am also extremely grateful to Arthur A. Houghton, Jr. for allowing me once again to publish miniatures from his marvelous *Shah-nama* and to his generously helpful assistant, Miss Sally Walker. Many friends and colleagues also deserve continuing gratitude: Annemarie Schimmel, Richard Ettinghausen, Marie Swietochowski, Ralph Pinder-Wilson, Peter Heath, Philip Hofer, Norah Titley, B. W. Robinson, John Rosenfield, Ivan Stchoukine, Basil Gray, Robert Skelton, Emel Essin, Jane Watts, Anthony Welch, Terence McInerney, Tatania Grek, Anatoli Ivanov, Mildred Frost, George Braziller, and Julianne deVere. As always, my wife and children have displayed remarkable forbearance in the midst of typing noises, mounds of color slides and photographs, and—worst of all—test readings aloud of prose snippets proclaimed by the author to be funny or enlightening.

Foreword

This is a "popular" book, not intended for the five or six specialists of Safavid art but for everyone. Hopefully, it will open many eyes to the deeper joys of Iranian painting, which too often is considered precious and slight. Our introduction omits documentation and footnotes. Those who want to learn more can do so by studying the books in the selected bibliography on page 29. (It should be noted that these paintings are often generally referred to as *Persian*, but throughout the text we will adhere to modern usage and call them *Iranian.*)

The pictures we have reproduced offer many moods. One evokes nostalgia (Plates 19, 20); others convey the delight of picnicking with a beloved or with friends (Plates 15, 43), the aristocratic pleasures of a great court (Plates 24, 26), or the rare sport of dragon slaying (Plate 9). Many simply tell diverting or instructive stories; and a few, such as Plate 4, appear to replay the antics of buffoons. But the miniatures we most warmly recommend are profoundly, elevatingly religious, though never pretentious or grim (Plates 2, 3, 18, 32, 33). Living with them could change your life!

S. C. W.

Contents

Introduction

These manuscripts were made to delight. To touch, gaze upon, or read, even to smell and hear the gentle rustle of their folios are pleasurable experiences. Connoisseurs of craftsmanship as well as of art can find much among their pages and bindings to astound and instruct. When these volumes were created whole workshops shared in the projects: makers of paper, specialists who burnished and cut the folios; others who measured and penned the razor-sharp rulings of the margins and colored and gilded them; experts who adorned chapter headings and other important passages with interlaces of arabesque and geometrical ornament in gold and color; artisans who spent their lives selecting and grinding pigments, most of which were made by pulverizing minerals such as gold, silver, lapis lazuli, and malachite—though some were derived from earths and secretions of beetles; chemically minded "scientists" who cooked up the binding media in secret (and still secret!) formulae of glues and, possibly, oils; lacquer and leather craftsmen who painted and tooled the sumptuous bindings; men who spent days sewing together the gathers; and librarians who supervised all these activities over the years required to fashion a great book. One cannot but be impressed by this small army of bibliophiles. And we have not yet listed the most crucial figures, the patrons, calligraphers, and artists—not to mention the authors of these literary classics.

Clearly, such manuscripts could only have been made for patrons whose wealth and power matched their appreciation of art and literature. The Safavid princes in sixteenth-century Iran were born and educated to such marvels. Earlier Iranian rulers (such as Il Khanids, Jala'irids, Turkmans, and Timurids) and Arab rulers before them had been munificent and discerning patrons of the arts of the book. Inasmuch as they spent much of their lives in the tents from which they hunted and fought, rather than in palaces, bulky possessions had little appeal. Their books, as a result, were often portable art galleries of small masterpieces. Prior to the late seventeenth century, when European influence became strong, pictures in oil technique on canvas were unknown in the Muslim world. The very large (wall paintings) and the very small (pictures for manuscripts and albums) were the rule. Meticulously worked volumes especially appealed to people who lived ruggedly most of their lives in bleak stretches of land occasionally relieved by flowers, trees, and other greenery. To them, handling such treasures must have been comparable to strolling in one of their lovingly tended walled gardens. Moreover, Muslims even more than Christians and Jews are "people of the book." It was not a great step from reading the

Prophet Muhammad's Holy *Qu'ran* to reading commentaries upon it, or lives of saints, or the works of Muslim historians or poets. As early as the tenth century A.D. Muslim bibliophiles were willing to pay huge sums for single pages of verses from the *Qu'ran* written by eminent scribes. Because of its relationship to the holy book, calligraphy was a major art—if not *the* major art—in the Islamic world. Over the centuries many different scripts were developed, from the dignified, powerful *Kufi* known from the many surviving *Qu'rans* copied on parchment (a material seldom used except in North Africa after the beginning of the eleventh century) to the more elegant *thuluth* and the refined, curvilinear *nasta'liq* in which these manuscripts were written with reed pens dipped into lustrous black ink.

For an Iranian artist of the sixteenth century, the peak of worldly success was recognition at the Shah's court and membership in the royal workshop, a virtual magnet to which exceptional artistic talent was drawn. If an apprentice painter in Shiraz revealed extraordinary ability, he was likely to be hired away from the bazaar workshop by the local governor, who would before long offer him to the Shah in the hopes of currying favor. Thus the young man of great talent would rise, like cream to the top of the milk bottle. Even the most humbly born in Safavid Iran could reach great heights. At least one imperial artist, Siyavush the Georgian, began as a slave boy captured during one of the Shah's western campaigns. Gifted as an artist and no doubt charming as well, he was apprenticed to the royal ateliers and eventually became one of Iran's major painters. This position would also have given him entrée to the imperial court, where the position of artists, like everything else in Safavid Iran, depended upon the Shah's good will. Aqa Mirak, one of the leading artists represented here (Plates 19, 20, 22, 23, 30, 31), was a boon companion of the Shah, particularly noted for his imperial portraits. Sultan-Muhammad, who was unquestionably the greatest of the Shah's artists (Plates 2–7, 13, 15, 17, 18, 21, 25, 32, 33) must have been less personally close to his master, though professionally he was even more warmly admired. His son, Muzaffar 'Ali (Plates 40, 45), was one of the leading Safavid painters of the second generation, and his particular gift was to record the psychological interplay of the Safavid nobility, no doubt the result of years of intimate association with court circles.

The training of a painter began early and was extremely thorough. Even Shah Tahmasp, a gifted amateur whose surviving works are skillfully painted and delightfully funny, must have toiled considerably to master an extremely demanding craft. For the professional, such training would have been yet more rigorous. In addition to mastering the essential social graces (i.e., Iranian literature, horsemanship, courtly etiquette, et al.), he had to learn to make brushes from kitten or baby squirrel hairs perfectly balanced and tied into quill handles, to grade and pulverize pigments, to prepare binding media, to use gold and silver paint, and much more. Far more important were lessons in drawing, a fundamental requirement for all painters. We envision small children, seated cross-legged on mats with drawing boards balanced on one knee and surrounded by little shells of ink and colors. Endlessly, they would copy their masters' formulae for dragons, flowering trees, elegant princesses, or stout-hearted warriors slaying horrible demons. Since Iranian painting is probably unrivaled in world art for the purity and intensity of its color, apprentices also had to discover the properties of each hue both separately and in conjunction with all the rest, for in Iranian miniatures the palette not only forms a visual "chord," like a cluster of musical notes, but also can be enjoyed bit by bit. It is a great pleasure, for instance, to look at a miniature for the pattern of blues, reds, or whites alone.

Perhaps the most characteristic element in Iranian painting is its use of arabesque, the rhythmic design based upon flowering vines that invigorates most Islamic art. Like a pulse, the reciprocal rhythms of this ornamental system suffuse and unify all Iranian compositions. Without it, these paintings would be as unthinkable as an orchestra playing a Bach suite without rhythm. With it, they are the visual equivalent of poetic verse.

Close observation of Safavid manuscripts shows that aspiring young artists contributed to them in minor ways, such as laying in flat areas of color. As their skills developed, more demanding (and interesting) passages were assigned. At the age of seventeen or so, a particularly able apprentice might have been given the task of coloring a whole miniature designed, or to use their term "outlined," by a master. This must have been a trying role for eager young artists who toiled for months on pictures that were credited to the master artists, whose work had taken far less time. In due course, however, the novices became masters; and it was their turn to train a further generation by assigning instructive if menial tasks. Moreover, if Iranian miniatures impress us with the time-consuming labor required to paint them, we are far more impressed by their artists' creative joy.

While such feelings of creative ecstasy were the artist's greatest reward, he also needed more tangible sustenance. In this respect, his earnings were commensurate with those of other members of the Shah's establishment—his military officers, musicians, butlers, and equerries. Like them, he received a salary as well as occasional bonuses, depending of course upon his patron's enthusiasm, or lack thereof. If a particularly exciting miniature was offered to the Shah when his mood was generous, the artist might have been favored with a richly embroidered coat of honor, a jeweled dagger, or even a village and the surrounding farmland. If the artist earned his royal master's disfavor, as did one unhappy painter who ran off with Shah Tahmasp's favorite page boy, he could expect terrible punishment. (In this case the artist's nose was severed by the Shah's own hand! But later he was forgiven; and soon he sported a new nose, carved by himself of wood and polychromed, shapelier than the original.)

If the Shah was Iran's leading patron, he was not the only one. While employed at court, royal artists augmented their incomes by illustrating humbler manuscripts for government officials or rich merchants; and if an artist lost favor with the Shah, he could either find employment at one of the commercial centers, such as the bazaars of Shiraz, or he could emigrate. During the sixteenth century, eager rivals at the courts of the Ottomans, the Uzbeks, the Mughals, or the sultans of the Deccan vied with the Safavids for men of talent.

The Safavid rulers for whom our manuscripts were made descended from a religious leader, Shaykh Safi al-Din, who died in 1334 A.D. after founding a brotherhood of dervishes near Ardabil on the Caspian Sea. By 1450, his heirs had added secular to religious power and become sultans of a military order. In 1501, at the age of fifteen, Isma'il inherited the Safavid leadership. Within a year he had defeated and killed Sultan Rustam, the Aq Qoyunlu Turkman who had ruled much of western Iran from his capital at Tabriz. But the dynamic young king was not yet satisfied in his quest for territory. After assuming the title of Shah, he set off upon further military campaigns. In 1503, he occupied Shiraz, a major Iranian city to the south, and in 1509 he defeated his eastern rivals, the Uzbeks, at the battle of Merv. A year later, he slew their ruler, Shaybani Khan, and took Herat, the former capital of the Timurids. By 1514, Shah Isma'il had survived an invasion of Tabriz by his enemies to the west, the Ottoman Turks with whom he reached at least a temporary accord, and had waged further, decisive campaigns against the Uzbeks. Having brought together eastern and western Iran, he now settled at Tabriz, where he remained for ten years until just before his death at the age of thirty-eight.

Shah Isma'il's personality was like that of many founders of great dynasties. Physically powerful, brave and lucky in battle, he was a charismatic leader whose rough Turkman soldiers would follow him anywhere. Earthy, intuitive, and warm-hearted, he could be ruthless and changeable. Consistency and logic were foreign to him. On the one hand he could write wildly heretical religious verse, declaring himself to be Jesus, Moses, or the evil Zahhak (see Plates 6, 7), while on the other he was ordering forged documents proving his religious orthodoxy and descent from the family of the Prophet.

He was related by marriage to the royal family of the Aq Qoyunlu Turkmans; and his childhood was spent within their cultural orbit. One can assume that he was familiar with the art of this Tabriz dynasty. A characteristic example is a bold drawing of dragons and phoenixes from an album assembled for Sultan Yaqub,

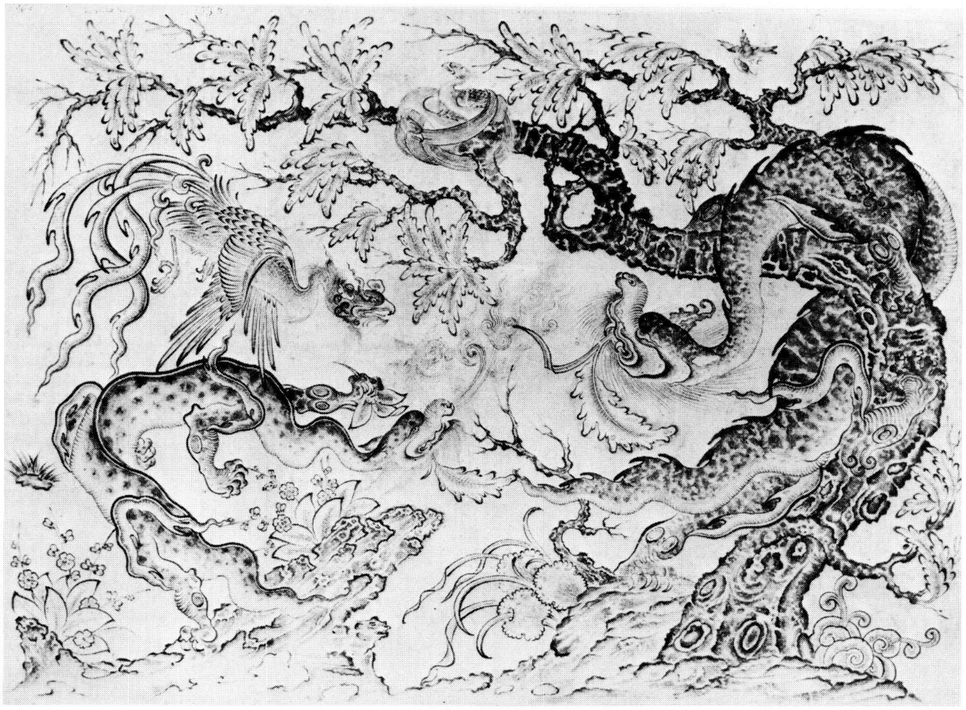

1. Drawing, Turkman School. Topkapi Saray Museum Library, Istanbul, Album H. 2153.

the Turkman ruler, and now in the library of the Topkapi Saray Museum in Istanbul (Figure 1). At once dramatic, humorous, and slightly scary, this picture of hungry beasts eager to chomp into a nest of baby birds invites a close look. The nubby bark of the tree, for instance, contains a secret cast of monsters and grotesques, creatures from a mystical and personal world that recalls Shah Isma'il's wilder verses. Significant, too, is the markedly Chinese character of the flowers, foliage, rocks, and monsters, motifs which owe their inspiration to the textiles, bronzes, pictures, and ceramics that were brought to the Turkman capital from the Far East.

When Shah Isma'il captured Tabriz, the spoils must have included this very drawing, along with vast numbers of others, and the fabulous royal library of the Turkman rulers. This great treasure would also have contained the accumulated manuscripts and miniatures of the earlier Tabriz rulers, the Mongols, Il Khanids, Jala'irids, and the Qara-Qoyunlu Turkmans. Moreover, the conqueror acquired the Tabriz workshops with their inheritance of "trade secrets," including drawings, tracings, and materials that had remained in the ateliers for many generations. Inasmuch as painters and other men of artistic ability brought delight and luster to a court, even the most bloodthirsty founders of new dynasties not only spared them but encouraged them to work for the new regime.

Art history and politics are in many ways inseparable; and the development of Safavid painting is consistent with Shah Isma'il's success as a warrior and statesman. Unlike his predecessors, the Turkmans, he ruled eastern as well as western Iran. As one might expect, the styles of his artists reflected this unification. The leading painter of eastern art was the renowned Bihzad, court artist to Sultan Husayn Mirza of Herat, the last of the Timurid rulers and one of Iran's most imaginative and discerning patrons. Along with his brilliant vizier, Mir 'Ali Shir Nawa'i (the author of the second manuscript treated here), he inspired artists, writers, and musicians to truly classical heights. A miniature by Bihzad from a *Bustan* of Sa'di dated 1488/89, now in the Egyptian National Library, Cairo, exemplifies this peak (Figure 2). Painted with infinite fineness, in subtly harmonious color, it describes the disturbing moment when Yusuf (Joseph of the Bible) was trapped by Zulaykha (Potiphar's wife) in a boudoir decorated with erotically tempting pictures. With saintly chastity, the beautiful young man escaped from his would-be seducer's apartment, shown as a mazelike structure of staircases and closed doors. Bihzad's genius dramatized the tale while also lavishing upon it a jeweler's dream of rich ornament. Every step or wall panel is beautified with geometrical and arabesque ornament. In spite of all this finery, the composition is spatially as logical and consistent as an architect's ground plan. While the spatially haphazard Turkman drawing (Figure 1) reaches out and grabs us in a flash, Bihzad's painting can only be comprehended by sustained contemplation.

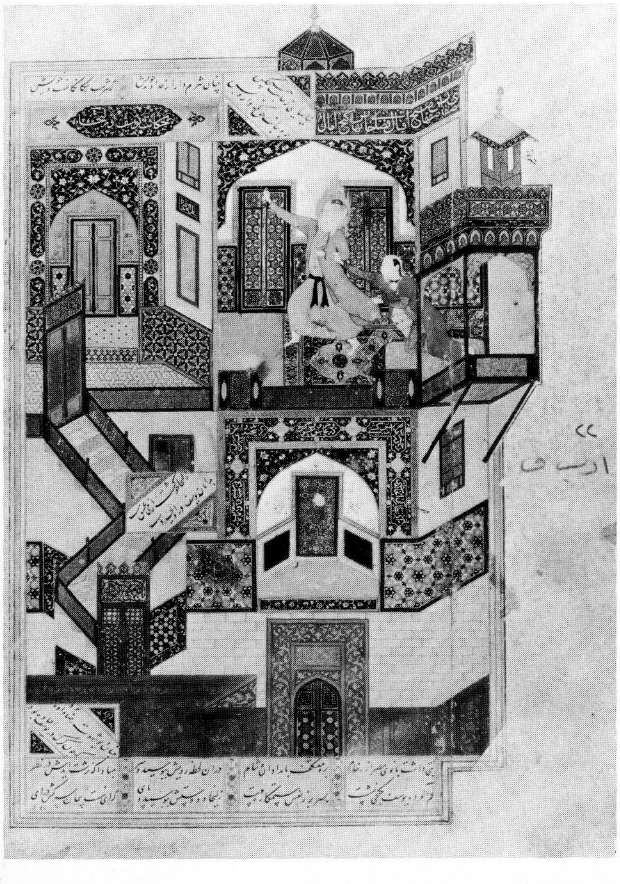

2. Miniature from a *Bustan* of Sa'di by Bihzad, 1488–89. Egyptian National Library, Cairo.

The synthesis of western and eastern Iran was furthered when Shah Isma'il sent his eldest son, at the age of only a few months, to be nominal governor of Herat in 1514. The infant prince was put in charge of a courtier named Qadi yi Jahan, whose attitudes towards life would have made him sympathetic to the artists and literati of Herat. Although Mir 'Ali Shir Nawa'i and Sultan Husayn were dead, Bihzad, the poet Hatifi, and many other luminaries of the former Timurid court lived on. As a cultural center, Herat had survived the conquests of both the Uzbeks in 1507 and 1513 and the Safavids in 1511 and 1514.

Growing up in Herat rather than Tabriz was significantly different for Prince Tahmasp. For one, it separated him from his parents. He never saw his dynamic and slightly raw father from the day he left Tabriz in 1514 until the day he returned, following a political upheaval in Herat, in 1522. His personality and artistic and literary tastes were shaped to the subtler, more elegant mode of the former Timurid capital, where manners were more refined than in Tabriz, which must have retained something of the flavor of Shah Isma'il's rough and tumble military campaigns. Iranian princes began their education very young, and Tahmasp would have been exposed thoroughly to the leading intellectuals and artists of Herat during his governorship. In all likelihood his father's enthusiasm for art in the Tabriz manner (Figure 1), as compared to that of Herat (Figure 2), must have seemed misguided and coarse. On the other hand, Shah Isma'il may well have lamented his son's effete Herati ways.

If so, both were diplomatic and tried to adjust to the other's personality. Since both were keen about painting, they probably spent many happy hours looking at manuscripts and planning new ones. Perhaps to please Prince Tahmasp, Shah Isma'il made Bihzad director of the royal library at this time. The venerable artist, who was no longer at the peak of his powers as a practicing painter, seems to have come to Tabriz when the Prince returned. In all probability the Houghton *Shah-nama* (Plates 1–10), though it contains the date 1527, was begun at this time, presumably as a present from the father to the son. Many of its earliest miniatures, such as Plate 4, *Hushang Slaying the Black Div* (demon), can be attributed to Sultan-Muhammad and his school, still working in the Tabriz manner of Figure 1. While such infectiously delightful pictures can only have charmed their elegant recipient, his penchant for more refined, subtler art soon prevailed. The greatest miniature in the manuscript, and probably the greatest picture in Iranian art, *The Court of Gayumarth* (Plates 2, 3), tempers the excessive visionary imagination of the Turkman tradition with the refined classicism of Herat. Although the rocks and clouds boil up with concealed grotesques, they are now painted with a fineness unprecedented in western Iran. *The Death of Zahhak* (Plate 6), a later miniature from the same manuscript, which was a major project of the royal ateliers for several decades, reveals Sultan-Muhammad's balanced synthesis of the two traditions. His concealed grotesques remain in both rocks and clouds, but they have now become far more naturalistic, and his treatment of space has taken on an almost Bihzadian logic. Stylistically, this miniature might almost belong to the *Khamsa* of Nizami of 1539–1543 (Plates 19–33) to which Sultan-Muhammad also contributed the most marvelous pictures.

The merging of the eastern and western styles did not, however, take place with timetable precision. Even Sultan-Muhammad, its most progressive exponent, reverted to his delightful earlier ways from time to time (Plates 13, 15, 17, 18), while his followers, such as an artist we know as Painter D (Plate 8), took far longer to adjust to the new idiom. Indeed, his vividly colorful painting of Zal being sighted by a caravan harks back to the drawing of dragons and phoenixes from Sultan Yaqub Beq's album (Figure 1).

Shah Isma'il died in 1524 while on a pilgrimage to Ardabil. It would be tempting to see his premature death as an assassination either by the Turkman tribesmen who had fought for him in the early days and whose power he had later tried to weaken or by the Herati faction represented by Prince Tahmasp's regent Qadi yi Jahan. But there is no proof that he was the victim of the strain accompanying a changing ethos. Whatever the cause of his father's death, Prince Tahmasp became Shah at the age of ten.

His position was far from enviable. Safavid Iran was by no means secure either internally or externally. The struggling factions at court scarcely heeded the young Shah, while the Ottomans to the west and the Uzbeks to the east sharpened their swords for war. In the meantime, the boy Shah found comfort in his books and pictures. He was already an accomplished calligrapher and his training as a painter was being furthered under the guidance of the great Sultan-Muhammad himself. His political torments were to some degree compensated for by the pleasures of art. During these years the young Shah must have greatly enjoyed the frequent discussions with the artists of his copiously illustrated *Shah-nama.*

One of the pleasures of directing the creation of great manuscripts must have been the differences between the projects. The format and style appropriate to a *Shah-nama*, for instance, would not do for a copy of Nawa'i's or Hafiz's or Jami's poetry. Thus, when a subject was chosen, the requirements of the poems to be copied, ornamented, illustrated, and bound had to be pondered. A particular calligrapher might have seemed the right one for the book at hand, while a certain artist's special talents demanded that he and only he be chosen.

Although we are not certain that it was prepared for Shah Tahmasp himself, the collected works in two volumes of the Timurid poet-statesman Mir 'Ali Shir Nawa'i was produced on the most royal level in 1526/27. It is now in the

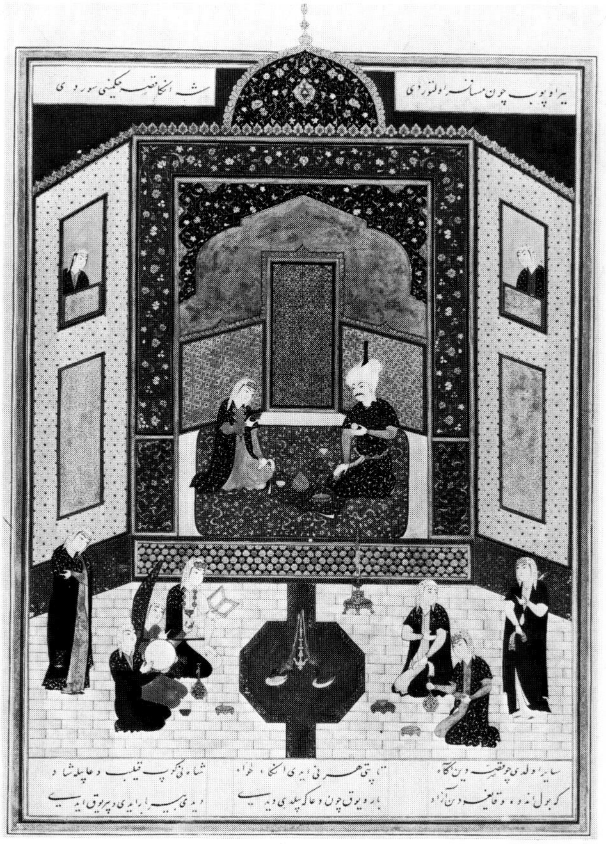

A

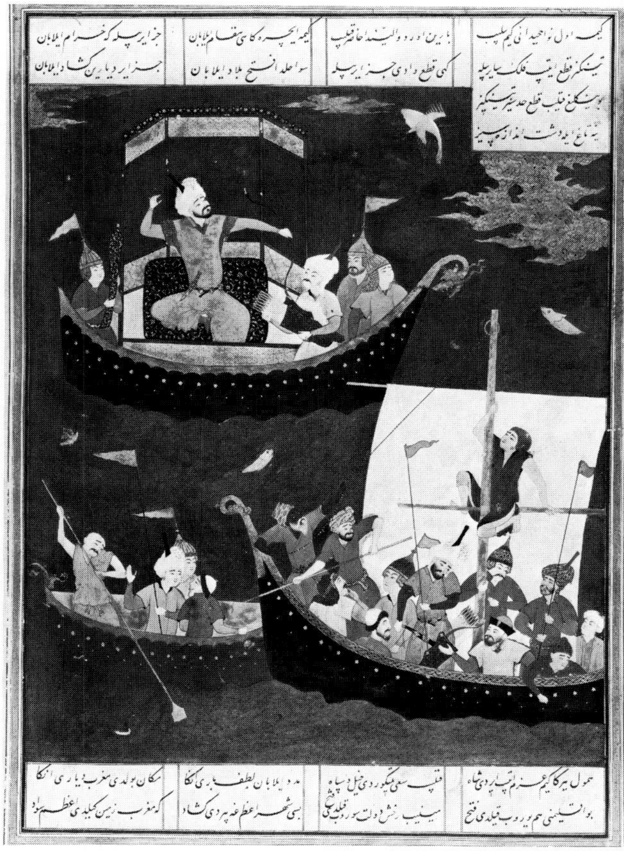

B

Bibliothèque nationale, Paris (supp. turc. 316, 317). In keeping with the author's Herat provenance, the volumes were written there by a famous scribe, 'Ali Hijrani. Both binding and illumination are in the classic Herat manner, and five of the six illustrations are attributable to Shaykh Zadeh, who more than any other painter perpetuated the formal elements of Bihzad's style. Above all, Shaykh Zadeh was a master of counterpoint, rhythm, and arabesque, to whom proportions and intricately related curves and angles meant more than human behavior. His pictures recall those of Poussin or Mondrian (Plates 11, 12, 14, Figure 2).

Our knowledge of Shaykh Zadeh rests almost entirely on his work. The sole literary reference to him was by Ali, an Ottoman man of letters. His style, however, is unmistakable and his influence upon other Safavid artists, particularly of the second generation, was considerable. We sense the participation of the young Mirza 'Ali and Muzaffar 'Ali in his illustrations to Nawa'i.

Sultan-Muhammad's single contribution to the Paris manuscript, *Bahram Gur Hunting before Azada* (Plate 13), interrupts Shaykh Zadeh's austere mood with laughter and humanity. Organically rather than architecturally composed, it is simultaneously serious and funny. Accompanied by his beloved but fickle Azada, Bahram Gur lets fly an arrow at a wild ass, whose turned head and toothy grin inspire wryly profound comments upon hunters and the hunted.

The ratio of Shaykh Zadeh's work to Sultan-Muhammad's changed in the *Diwan* of Hafiz, a slightly later manuscript (ca. 1527) to which the former contributed two and the latter five miniatures. (Regrettably, Shaykh Zadeh's polo scene, Figure c, was stolen from the book during World War II and is now lost.) One of Sultan-Muhammad's miniatures, *The Feast of 'Id Begins* (Plate 17), is inscribed with the name of Sam Mirza, one of Shah Tahmasp's brothers, and it was probably made for him, perhaps as a present from the Shah. The young prince seated on the throne bearing one of the two known signatures of Sultan-Muhammad (the other is on Plate 18) is generally accepted as a portrait of Sam Mirza, the most literary of the Shah's brothers, who wrote important accounts of contemporary poets. Although at least one other major illustrated manuscript was made by the royal workshop for Sam Mirza (Jami's *Chain of Gold*, now in the State Library, Leningrad), he was not much loved by his reigning brother. Sam Mirza was implicated in a grave plot against the crown in 1535, so it is no wonder that the Shah eventually imprisoned him. Sam was killed in an earthquake in 1567.

However questionable his political loyalties may have been, Sam Mirza was unquestionably a man of great artistic and literary understanding for whom Shaykh Zadeh and Sultan-Muhammad worked with particular zeal. For this *Diwan* of Hafiz, the outstanding illustrated copy of the great Sufi poet's work, Shaykh Zadeh painted his most ambitious and successful picture, *Scandal in a Mosque* (Plate 16), a kaleidoscopic arrangement of refulgent color designed with the strength of architecture and enriched with some of the most refined and elegant arabesques in all Islamic painting. Here, he even succeeded in creating lively people, perhaps spurred on by the challenge of Sultan-Muhammad, or in response to the demands of his patron. Inasmuch as this Herat-minded artist was temperamentally unable to adjust to the new synthesis based on Turkman as well as Timurid sources, he moved to the Uzbek court of Bukhara, where his variant of Bihzad's style established a whole new school of painting.

Sultan-Muhammad's three miniatures for the *Diwan* are perfectly matched to the spirit and letter of Iran's greatest Sufi poet. The unsigned *Lovers Picnicking* (Plate 15) represents the romantic passion of Hafiz's mysticism, with its fiery oranges and glowing blues beneath a canopy of wind-driven arabesque, wild as lust. Even more imbued with the visionary Sufi spirit is his *Worldly and Otherworldly Drunkenness* (Plate 18) which demolishes the conventional split between the effects of wine and divine ecstasy. In this extraordinary transcen-

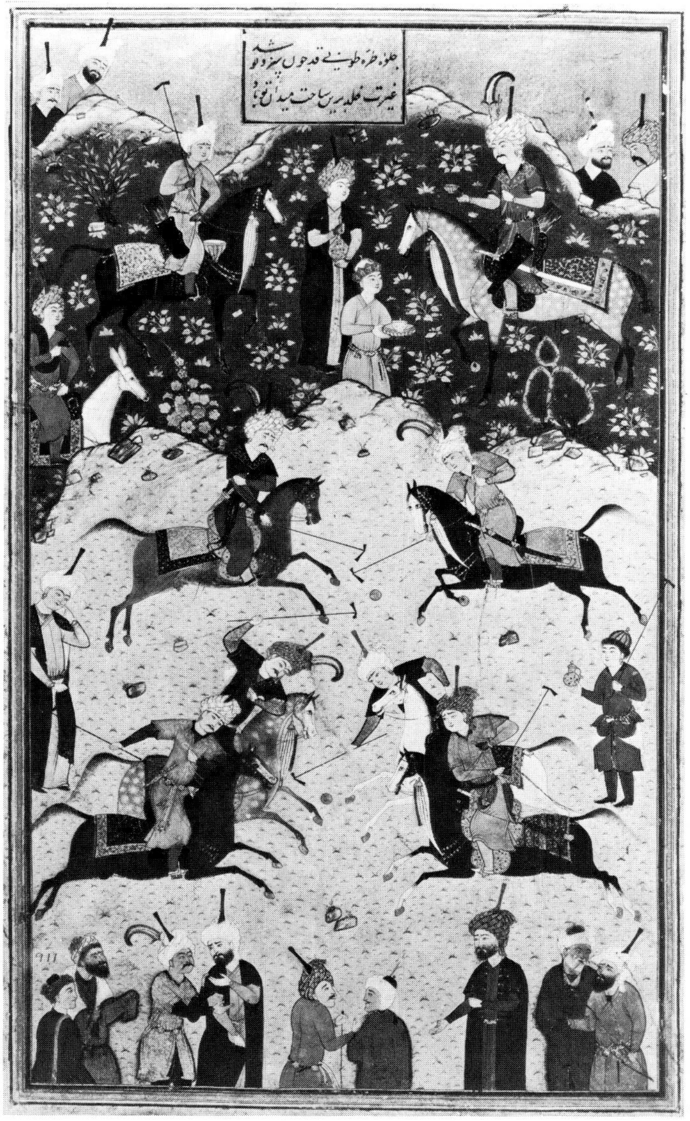

C

dental painting, low comedy and high religion meet. Slapstick comedians achieve sainthood; crazy laughter becomes prayer.

Sultan-Muhammad's *Worldly and Otherworldly Drunkenness* may have been his last overtly wild religious picture. The ethos of Safavid Iran was changing. In the beginning, Shah Isma'il's heretical fervor set the pace; but soon even he turned towards the orthodoxy that continued to gain ground throughout Tahmasp's reign. In 1533 Shah Tahmasp renounced all forbidden things, from fornication and hashish to wine. Prone to dreams, the Shah acted upon their messages. In 1536 he closed down the wine shops and brothels. Pleasures were equated with sin.

Fortunately, Shah Tahmasp's joy in painting survived long enough for at least one more manuscript, the justly renowned *Khamsa* of Nizami, which contains dates from 1539 to 1543. In its present state it contains fourteen contemporary miniatures and three late seventeenth-century ones, added along with many new borders when the volume was refurbished due to excessive wear and tear. Most of the major court artists painted for it: Sultan-Muhammad, Aqa Mirak, Mir Sayyid 'Ali, Mirza 'Ali, and Muzaffar 'Ali. By the time it was finished, the coming together of the Turkman and Timurid strains was complete. The earthy yet heavenly Turkman spirits, however, are still apparent through the naturalistic finesse and psychological portraiture derived from Bihzad. Sultan-Muhammad, the Sufi painter-saint, could no longer work with the flagrant intensity of earlier times. Wisely and brilliantly, he had adjusted to the Shah's increasingly orthodox mood, like a once outré holy man now dressed as a courtier. But underneath this new garb, he remained unchanged; and underneath the subtler, more naturalistic forms of his miniatures, Sultan-Muhammad's mystical spirit lived on, perhaps with increased intensity. A close look at any of his pictures for the *Khamsa* (Plates 21, 25, 32, 33) reveals that his secret cast of earth spirits continued to peep out from rocks and tree stumps.

Such creatures were no longer acceptable to the new generation of Safavid painters, whose juvenilia and first mature works are found in the Houghton *Shah-nama* (Plates 9, 10). By now these grotesques were equated with the superstitions, back-slapping, and coarse soldiery of Shah Isma'il. These former heroes were now dismissed as eccentrically vulgar old geezers. Sultan-Muhammad's own son, Mirza 'Ali, went so far as to caricature one of them as a craggy-faced curmudgeon wearing an old-fashioned thick-batoned turban in his miniature of *Nushaba Recognizing Iskandar from His Portrait.* (He is seen whispering to a courtier near the fence at the right side of the picture in Plate 24). To fully appreciate Mirza 'Ali's miniature, one must be prepared to explore gather-

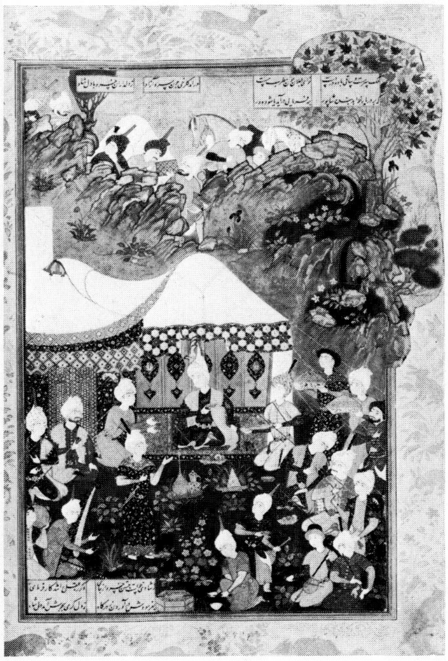

D

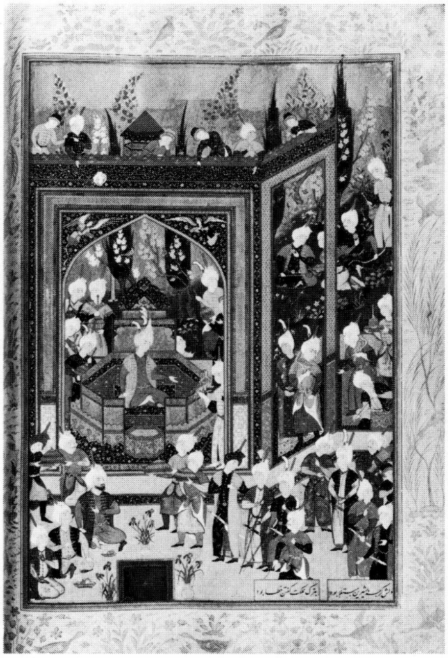

E

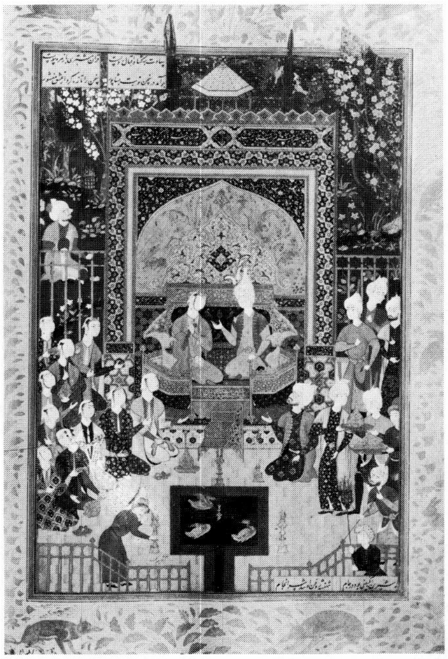

F

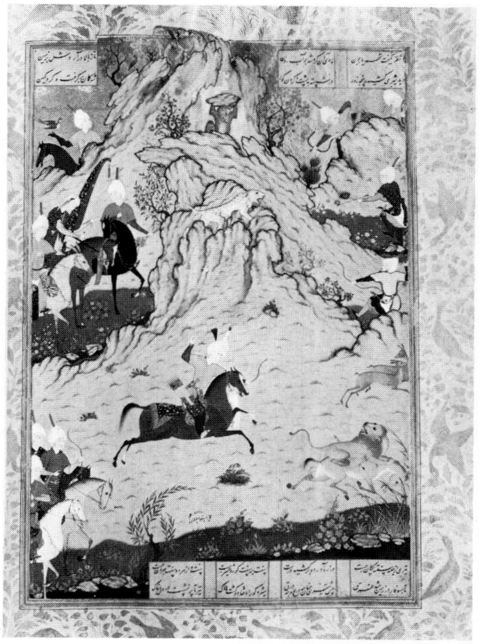

G

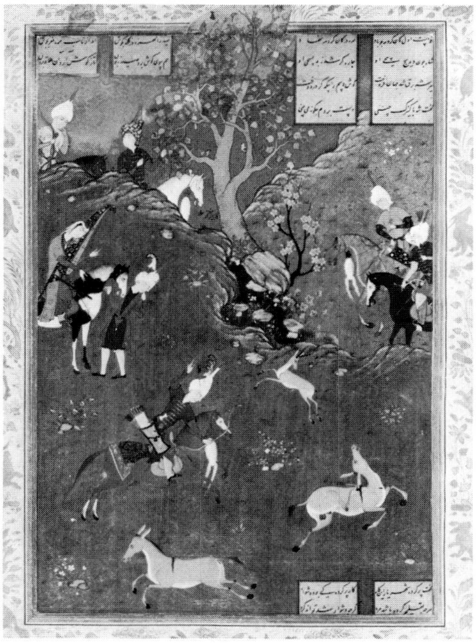

H

ings comparable to those in Sheridan's drawing rooms or Proust's salons. While his father was a holy man who painted spirits, he was an aristocrat who painted people; and he did so with a chef's knowledge of gastronomy, a fop's apprecia-tion of tailoring, and a psychiatrist's insight into mankind.

Not long after the completion of the British Museum *Khamsa*, Shah Tah-masp's guilt-inspired dreams and unsettling feelings of political responsibility caused him to turn away from painting. One wonders how his once honored and busy artists felt. Perhaps Sultan-Muhammad died of shock or, more likely, put down his brushes and took up an ascetic life. At any rate, we know of no pictures by him later than his *The Ascent of the Prophet to Heaven* (Plates 32, 33) in which Muhammad rides the human-headed Buraq through the skies. Angels (and viewers of the miniature) can gaze down through heavenly flames and still dragonish clouds at the orb of earth, thanks to the artist's realization of a true vision. We cannot imagine a greater Muslim religious painting.

A few artists, such as Aqa Mirak, the Shah's friend, carried on at Tabriz and later Qazvin. Others found patronage with the princes; and at least four painters (Mir Musavvir, Mir Sayyid 'Ali, Dust Muhammad, and Abd al Samad) left for the court of Humayun, the Mughal emperor.

By 1556, another major patron of painting inspired artists to create new won-ders. He was Ibrahim Mirza, then sixteen years old and the nephew of Shah Tahmasp. His father, Bahram Mirza, another connoisseur of pictures, was the Shah's favorite brother and the only one born of the same mother. Ibrahim seems to have combined his grandfather Isma'il's dynamism and magnetism with his uncle the Shah's aesthetic perfectionism. In spite of his stern Puritanism, Shah Tahmasp clearly doted on this nephew, whom he appointed governor of Mashhad in 1556 and to whom he gave one of his daughters in marriage. He even turned over to him the remaining royal artists. But his feelings toward Ibrahim were at times bitterly ambiguous. In his good moods the Shah could enjoy pleasures he denied himself, vicariously, through Ibrahim; in bleak ones he begrudged them. Unlike his uncle, Ibrahim was a free spirit, innocently delighting in art, poetry, music, polo, and science. Occasionally, he was foolishly undiplomatic, as when he earned his uncle's displeasure by giving sanctuary to a musician who had fled the Shah's wrath. In 1565 Ibrahim's governorship was revoked. Worse still, he was deprived of the use of the royal painters and calligraphers. From Mashhad he was moved to the small town of Sagzivar—a virtual Siberia. Fortunately, the Shah relented before he died and invited Ibrahim to return to the capital (now Qazvin) as an important official. Surviving miniatures of this period suggest that the aging, mellowed Shah and his favorite nephew jointly encouraged artists to illustrate several splendid manuscripts before Shah Tahmasp's death at sixty-two in 1576. A year later, alas, Ibrahim was murdered at thirty-eight by order of Shah Isma'il II, an old enemy who had inherited his father's throne. The first phase of Safavid painting had ended.

The *Haft Awrang* of Jami, now in the Freer Gallery of Art, was begun in 1556, when Ibrahim Mirza was appointed governor of Mashhad, and completed in 1565, the year he was replaced by the man who later ordered his death. Its twenty-eight unsigned miniatures can be attributed on stylistic grounds to many of the artists who worked on the Houghton *Shah-nama*: Mirza 'Ali, Muzaffar 'Ali, Shaykh Muhammad, Painters A and D, and Aqa Mirak. While some of the older artists such as Aqa Mirak probably remained in the Safavid capital and sent their miniatures by messenger to Ibrahim, the others must have lived in Mashhad.

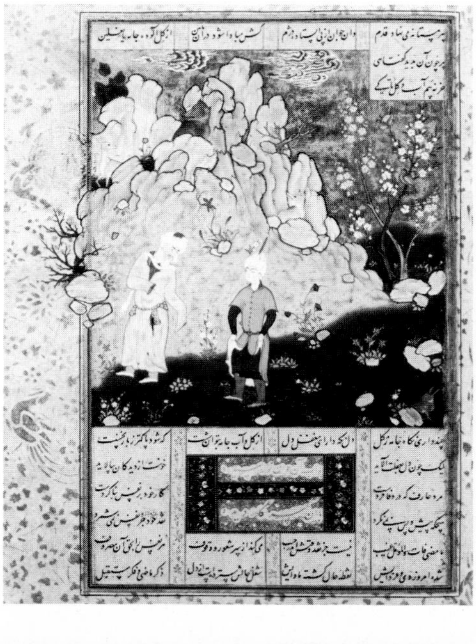

I

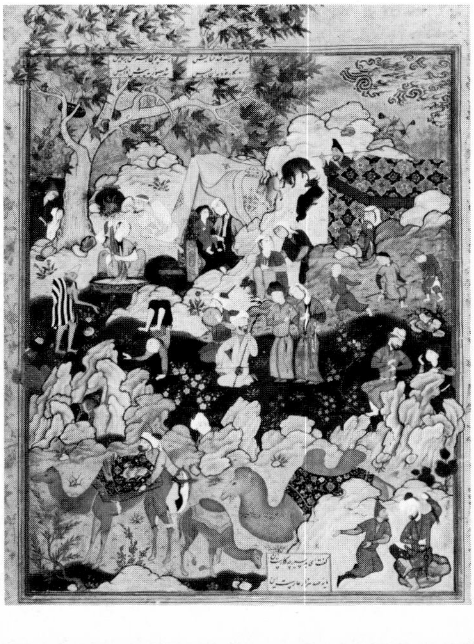

J

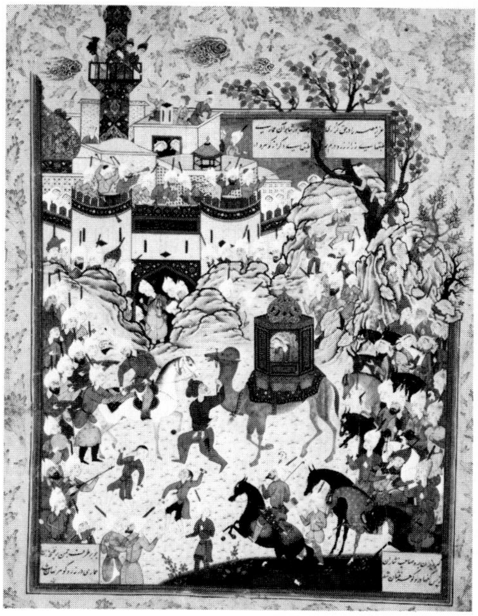

K

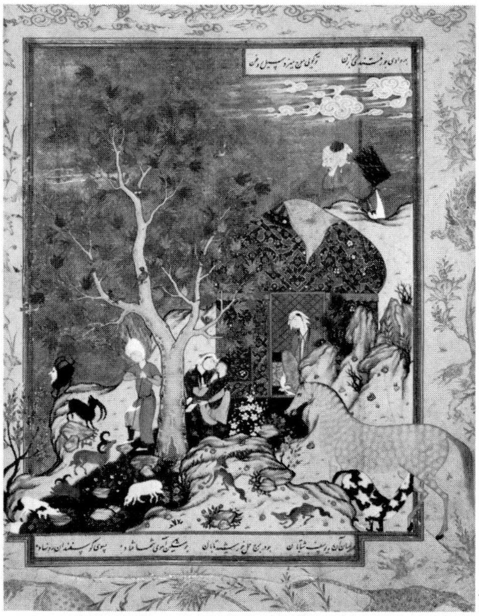

L

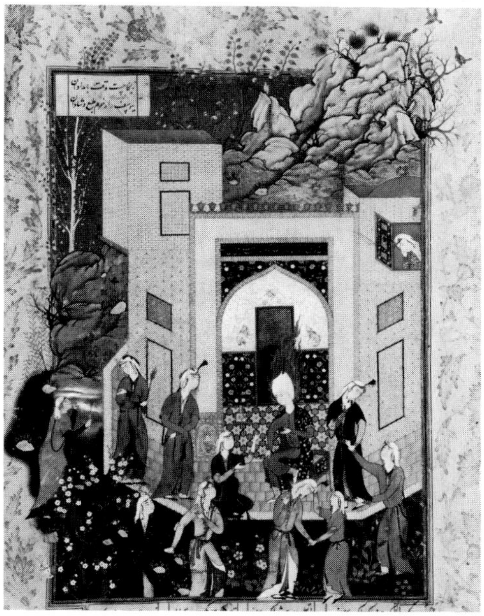

M

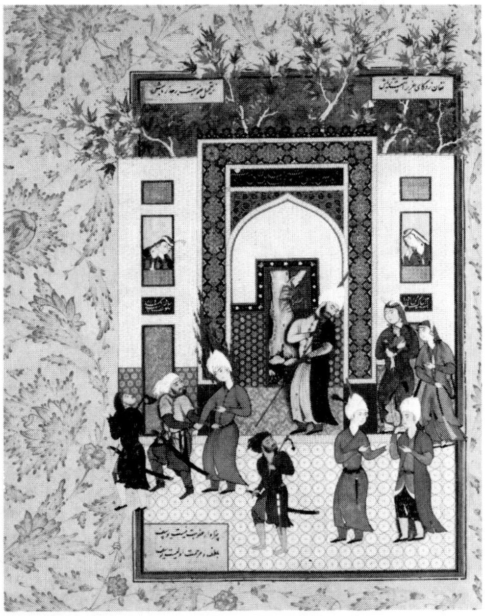

N

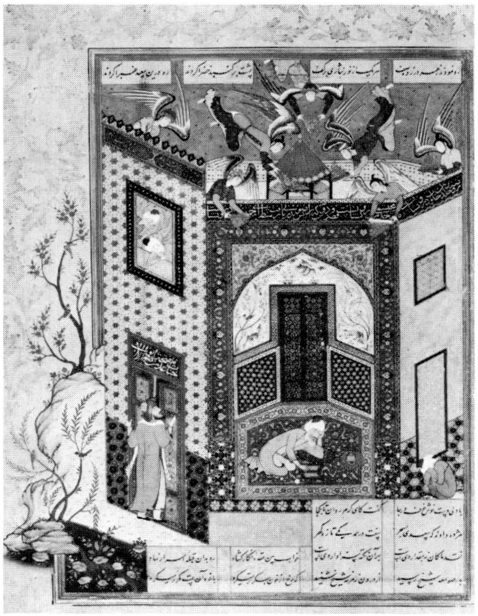

O

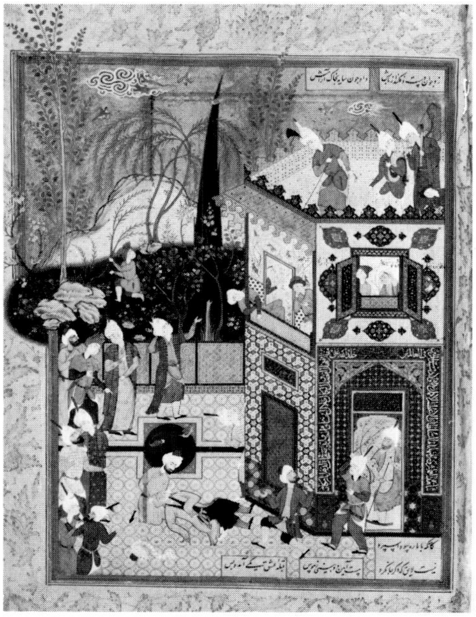

P

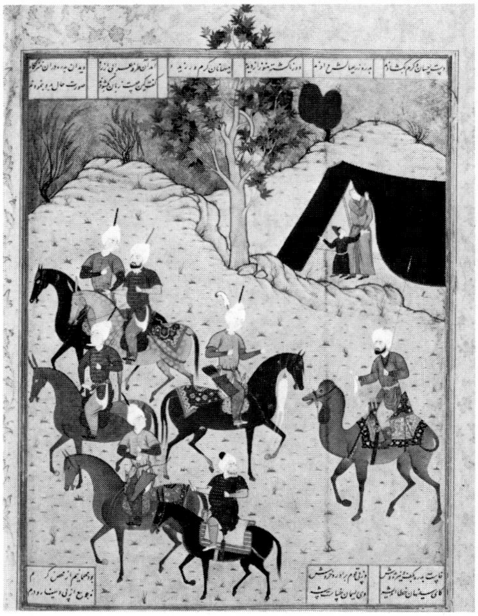

Q

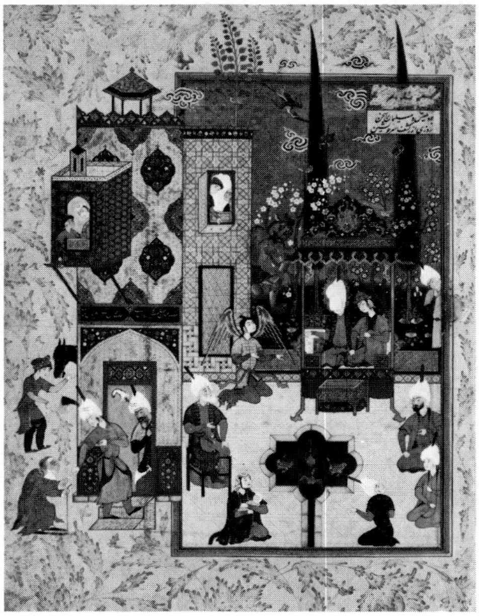

R

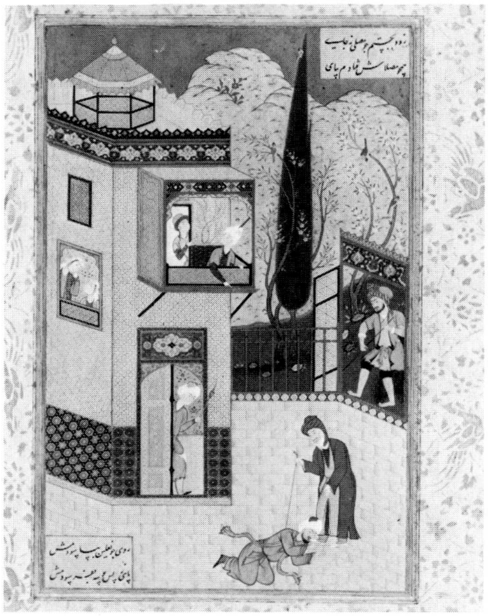

S

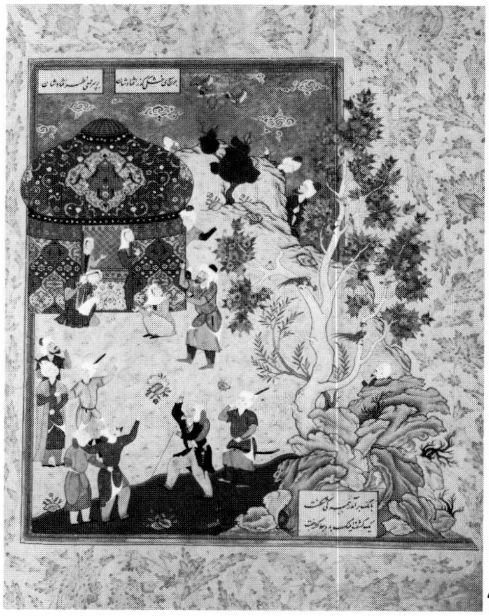

T

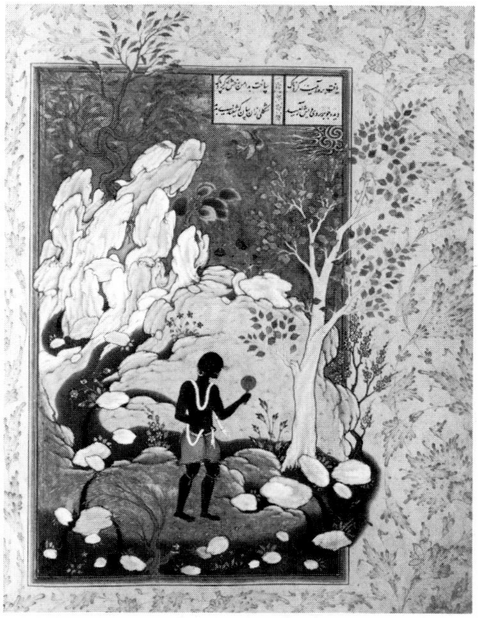

U

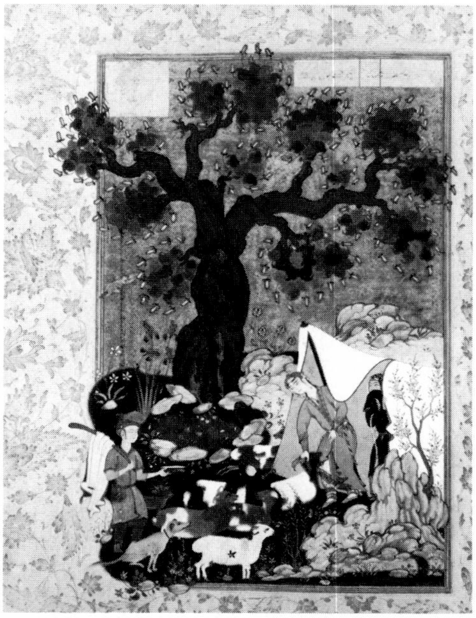

V

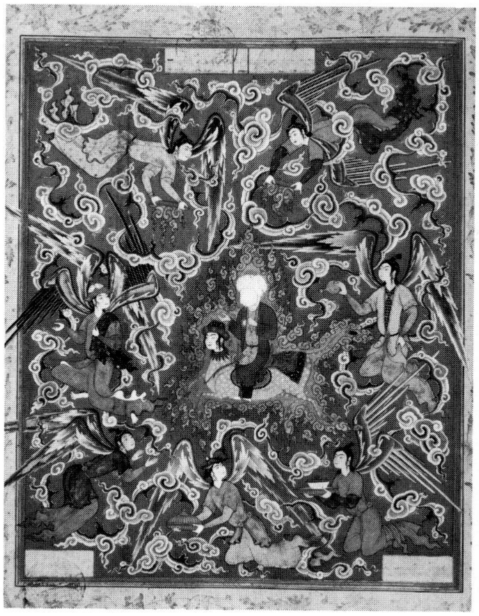

W

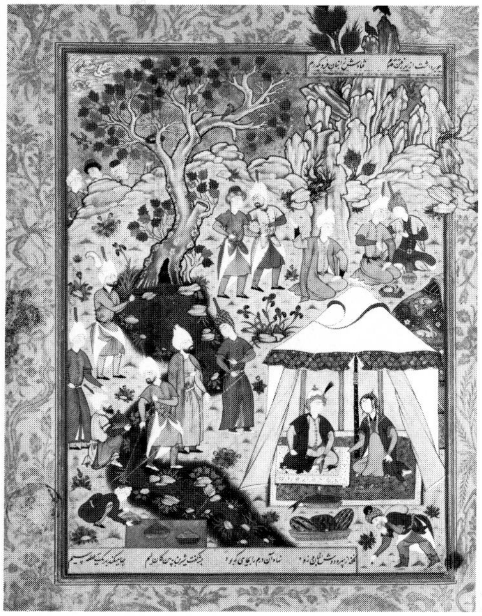

X

Since much of the success of such a project depended upon the partnership between patron and artist, it is perhaps not surprising that Aqa Mirak's two pictures for the *Haft Awrang* (Figures q and x) seem tame and somewhat dull. His greatest works, such as *Nushirvan Listening to the Owls on the Ruined Palace* (Plates 19, 20), were inspired by his friend the Shah, not by Ibrahim Mirza, whom he probably considered a troublesome, rather decadent young man. Mirza 'Ali's contributions to this manuscript, however, show that he could change with the times. His *Another Inadequate Gift* (Plate 42), with its slitheringly suggestive rocks and undulating rhythms, is attuned to Ibrahim's sensuously *louche* court. Another artist, Shaykh Muhammad, who had been little older than a boy when he worked on the Houghton manuscript, became the most dazzling if at times disturbing painter of the *Haft Awrang.* His most characteristic miniature, *Majnun Eavesdrops on Layla's Camp* (Plates 46, 47), is also the most admired in the book and probably the one which most accurately reflects the spirit of the artist, the patron, and the court. In it the usual moral values are reversed, recalling Shah Isma'il's paradoxical claim that he was the villainous Zahhak (see Plates 6, 7, and page 44). Here, the lovely Layla resembles a sullied courtesan; and all the other figures and animals seem to have stepped out of a nightmare or a blue movie. The composition, too, is upsetting, with its flapping rhythms, like a huge windmill breaking up in a hurricane. Gaudy with stripes, arabesques, and tooled gold, this miniature is rich as a fruitcake. Tasting such a confection could prove nauseous—but we should bear in mind that when the need is great catharsis becomes ecstasy. You can only know the heights if you have seen the depths.

Selected Bibliography

1. ARNOLD, SIR T. *Painting in Islam.* Oxford, 1928
2. BINYON, L. *The Poems of Nizami.* London, 1928
3. BINYON, L., Wilkinson, J. V. S., and Gray, B. *Persian Miniature Painting.* London, 1931
4. BLOCHET, E. *Les Enluminures des manuscrits orientaux de la Bibliothèque nationale.* Paris, 1926
5. BLOCHET, E. *Les Peintures des manuscrits orientaux de la Bibliothèque nationale.* Paris, 1914–20
6. BROWNE, E. G. *A Literary History of Persia.* Cambridge, 1951
7. DICKSON, M. B., and WELCH, S. C. *The Houghton Shah-nama.* Cambridge, Massachusetts (forthcoming)
8. GRAY, B. *Persian Painting.* Skira (Treasures of Asia), 1961
9. MARTIN, F. R. *The Miniature Painting and Painters of Persia, India, and Turkey.* London, 1912
10. ROBINSON, B. W. *A Descriptive Catalogue of the Persian Paintings in the Bodleian Library.* Oxford, 1958
11. RYPKA, J. *History of Iranian Literature.* Dordrecht, 1956
12. SAKISIAN, A. B. *La Miniature persane du XIIe au XVIIe siècle.* Paris and Brussels, 1929
13. SCHIMMEL, A. *Islamic Calligraphy.* Leiden, 1970
14. SCHROEDER, E. *Persian Miniatures in the Fogg Museum of Art.* Cambridge, Massachusetts, 1942
15. STCHOUKINE, I. *Les Peintures des manuscrits Safavis de 1502 à 1587.* Paris, 1959
16. WELCH, S. C. *A King's Book of Kings.* New York and London, 1972

List of Illustrations

In the following list the first number shown is the Plate number; the second is the folio of the actual manuscript; and the last number, italicized, is the page number in this volume. The lowercase letters (a, b, etc.) refer to figure numbers of the smaller black-and-white illustrations in the text.

The *Shah-nama*, "Book of Kings," the Iranian national epic; written by Abu'l-Qasim Mansur FIRDAWSI of Tus (born ca. 934, died ca. 1025); this copy in the library of Arthur A. Houghton, Jr., who presented 78 of its 258 miniatures to the Metropolitan Museum of Art, New York; scribes unknown, dated on a miniature, folio 516 verso 1527/28; folios measure 47.3 x 17.0 cm. Probably begun in 1522 as a present from Shah Isma'il to his eldest son, Prince Tahmasp, who continued the project into the 1530s or later. See Bibliography, Nos. 7, 16.

Collected Works of Mir 'Ali Shir Nawa'i (born ca. 1440/41, died 1501), in Chaghatai Turkish; Paris, Bibliothèque nationale, supp. turc 316, 317; copyist Ali Hijrani "at Herat" in 1526–27; six miniatures, size 38.0 x 26.5 cm. See Bibliography, Nos. 4, 5.

Diwan, "Collected Works," of Shams al-Din Muhammad HAFIZ (born ca. 1326, died 1390), Iran's greatest mystical poet; courtesy of the Fogg Museum of Art, Harvard University; scribe unknown; ca. 1527; four (once five) miniatures, two of them signed by Sultan-Muhammad, one signed by Shaykh Zadeh; folios 28.9 x 17.8 cm.; text area including rulings 19.7 x 13.2 cm.; probably made for Prince Sam Mirza, a younger brother of Shah Tahmasp. See Bibliography, Nos. 3, 7, 16.

The *Khamsa*, "Quintet," of Ilyas b. Yusuf NIZAMI (born ca. 1140/41, died 1202/03); British Museum (OR. 2265); copyist Mahmud al-Nishapuri; dated 1539–43; 14 contemporary miniatures, many with reliable attributions to painters, one with a semilegible contemporary attribution to Aqa Mirak; 3 miniatures added in the late seventeenth century by Muhammad Zaman; size 36.8 x 25.4 cm. See Bibliography, Nos. 2, 7.

The Haft Awrang, "The Seven Thrones," of Maulana Nuru'd Din Abdu'r-Rahman JAMI (born 1414, died 1492); The Freer Gallery of Art, Washington, D.C. (46.12); copyists Malik al-Daylami "at Mashhad," Shah Mahmud Nishapuri "at Mashhad," Rustam 'Ali, and Muhibb 'Ali; 28 miniatures, all unsigned an dunattributed; dated 1556–1565; size 34.2 x 23.2 cm.; made for Sultan Ibrahim Mirza (ca. 1540–1577), nephew of Shah Tahmasp. See Bibliography, No. 7.

Plates and Commentaries

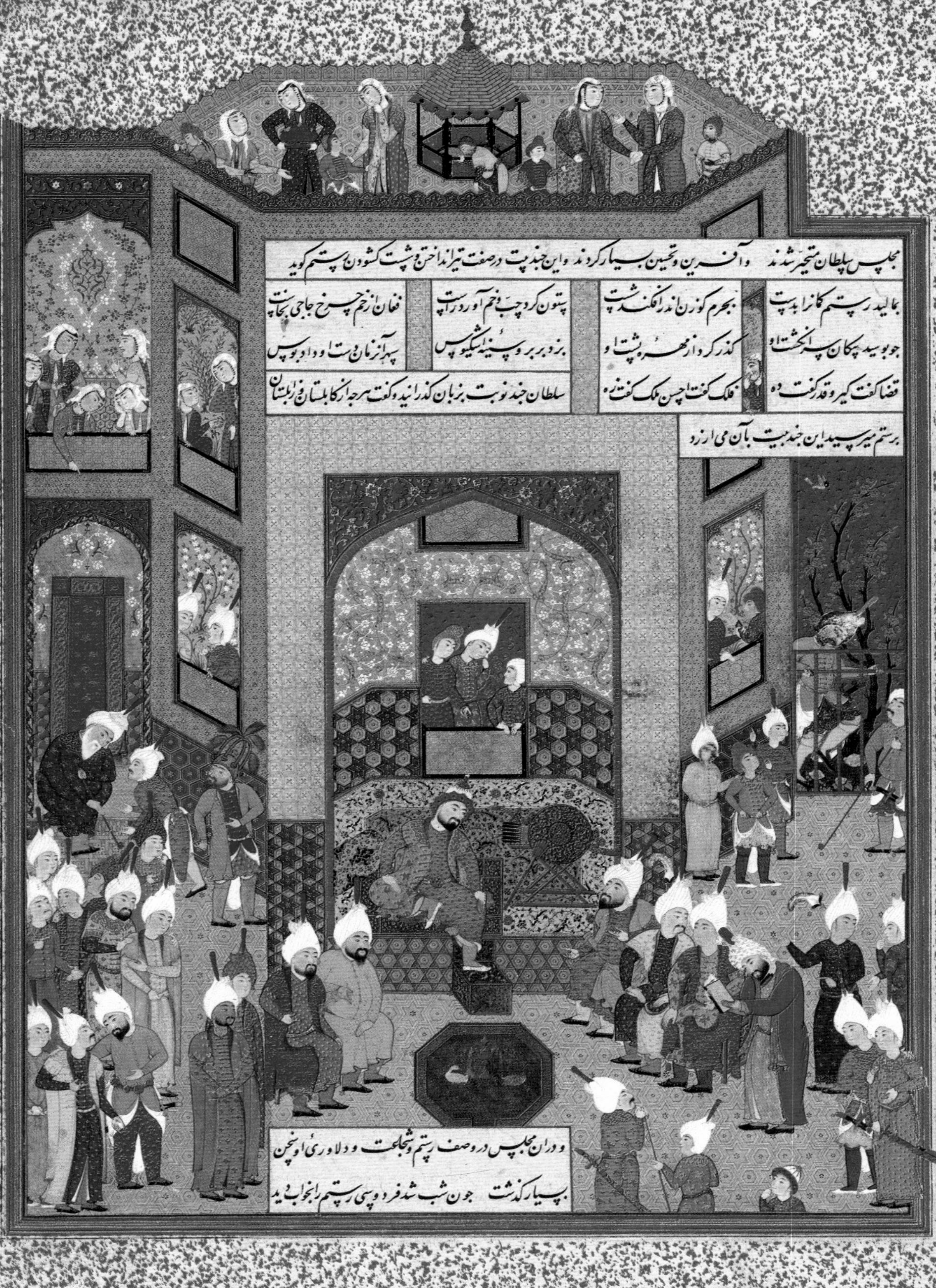
مجلس سلطان متحیر شدند و آفرین و تحسین بسیار کردند و این چند بیت در صفت تیر انداختن و شست کشودن رستم گوید
بمالید رستم کمان را بدست
بچرم گوزن اندر افکند شست
چو بوسید پیکان سر انگشت او
گذر کرد از مهره پشت او
قضا گفت گیر و قدر گفت ده
فلک گفت احسن ملک گفت زه
ستون کرد چپ و خم آورد راست
فغان از خم چرخ چاچی بخاست
بزد بر بر و سینه اشکبوس
سپهر آن زمان دست او داد بوس
سلطان چند نوبت بزبان گذرانید و گفت هر چه از کابلستان و زابلستان
برستم میرسید این چند بیت بآن می ارزد
و دران مجلس در وصف رستم و شجاعت و دلاوری او سخن
بسیار گذشت چون شب شد فردوسی رستم را بخواب دید

The Shah-nama of Firdawsi

PLATE 1, folio 10 recto*

Firdawsi Proves His Literary Talents at the Court of Sultan Mahmud of Ghazna

ATTRIBUTED TO MIR MUSAVVIR

An illustration to the introduction to the *Shah-nama* composed for the Timurid prince, Baisunqur, this picture shows the author demonstrating his literary prowess before his fickle patron, Sultan Mahmud of Ghazna. Mir Musavvir, one of the three senior artists of this great volume, is notable for his gently flowing line, pleasing characterizations, generously rounded arabesques, and harmoniously inventive colors. Costumes and settings, as usual in Iranian painting, are idealized from contemporary life rather than being reconstructions of the period they illustrate.

* Because Iranian manuscripts are read from right to left, "rectos" are left-hand pages.

PLATE 2, folio 20 verso

The Court of Gayumarth

ATTRIBUTABLE TO* SULTAN-MUHAMMAD

Gayumarth was the legendary first Shah of Iran, and his reign was idyllic until the demon (div) Ahriman plotted against him, thereby introducing evil to a world hitherto innocent. Although the angel Surush (left, standing on a mountain crag) warned Gayumarth of impending trouble, the Shah's son Siyamak was slain in a battle against the Black Div, son of Ahriman.

This miniature is the supreme masterpiece of the Houghton *Shah-nama*, if not of all Iranian painting. It was painted by Sultan-Muhammad, the leading artist of both Shah Isma'il and of his son, Prince Tahmasp, who was largely responsible for the synthesis of the western (Tabriz) and eastern (Herat) traditions during the early Safavid period. Although unsigned, this painting can be attributed on the basis of comparison to Sultan-Muhammad's only two signed works (Plates 17, 18) and a contemporary description of it by a fellow artist, Dust Muhammad, in the introduction to an album assembled for Shah Tahmasp's brother, Bahram Mirza (Topkapi Saray Museum Library, H. 2154). For other miniatures by Sultan-Muhammad, see Plates 4–7, 14, 15, 17, 18, 21, 25, 32 and 33, and Figure g.

* "Attributable to" is used to designate new attributions made by the author. "Attributed to" signifies acceptance of the traditional attributions.

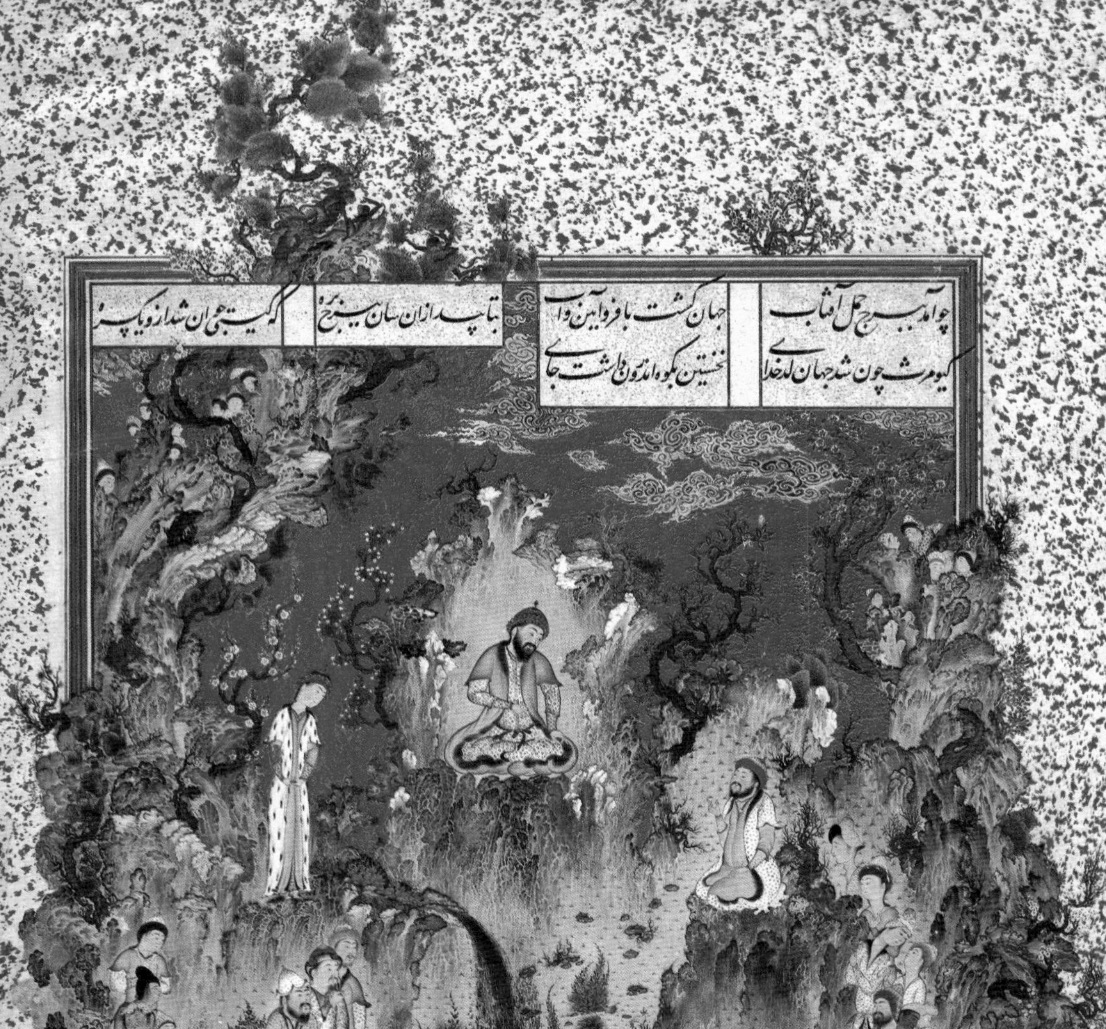

چو آمد ببرج حمل آفتاب
جهان گشت با فر و آیین و آب
بتابید ازان سان ز برج بره
که گیتی جوان شد ازو یکسره
کیومرث چون شد جهان کدخدای
نخستین بکوه اندرون داشت جای
سر تاج و تختش بر آمد ز کوه
پلنگینه پوشید خود با گروه
ازو اندر آمد همی پرورش
که پوشیدنی نو بد و نو خورش

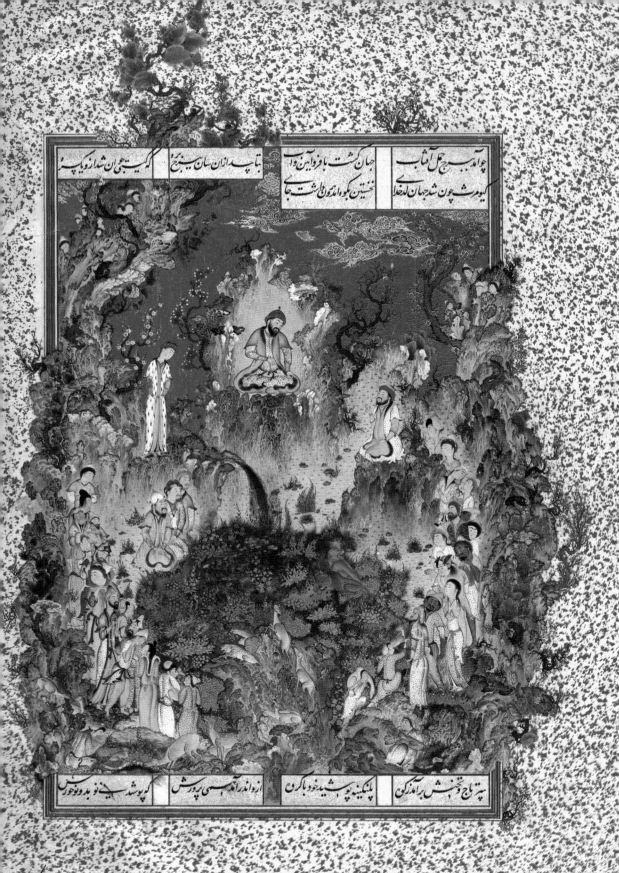

PLATE 3, folio 20 verso

The Court of Gayumarth/detail, *Courtiers, landscape, and animals*

ATTRIBUTABLE TO SULTAN-MUHAMMAD

One of Sultan-Muhammad's most profound and captivating characteristics is his tendency to inhabit rocks, clouds, and tree stumps with hidden personages and animals. At times these are more naturalistically portrayed than the principal players in his illustrations. Although their precise significance cannot be known, they appear to be mystically inspired earth spirits.

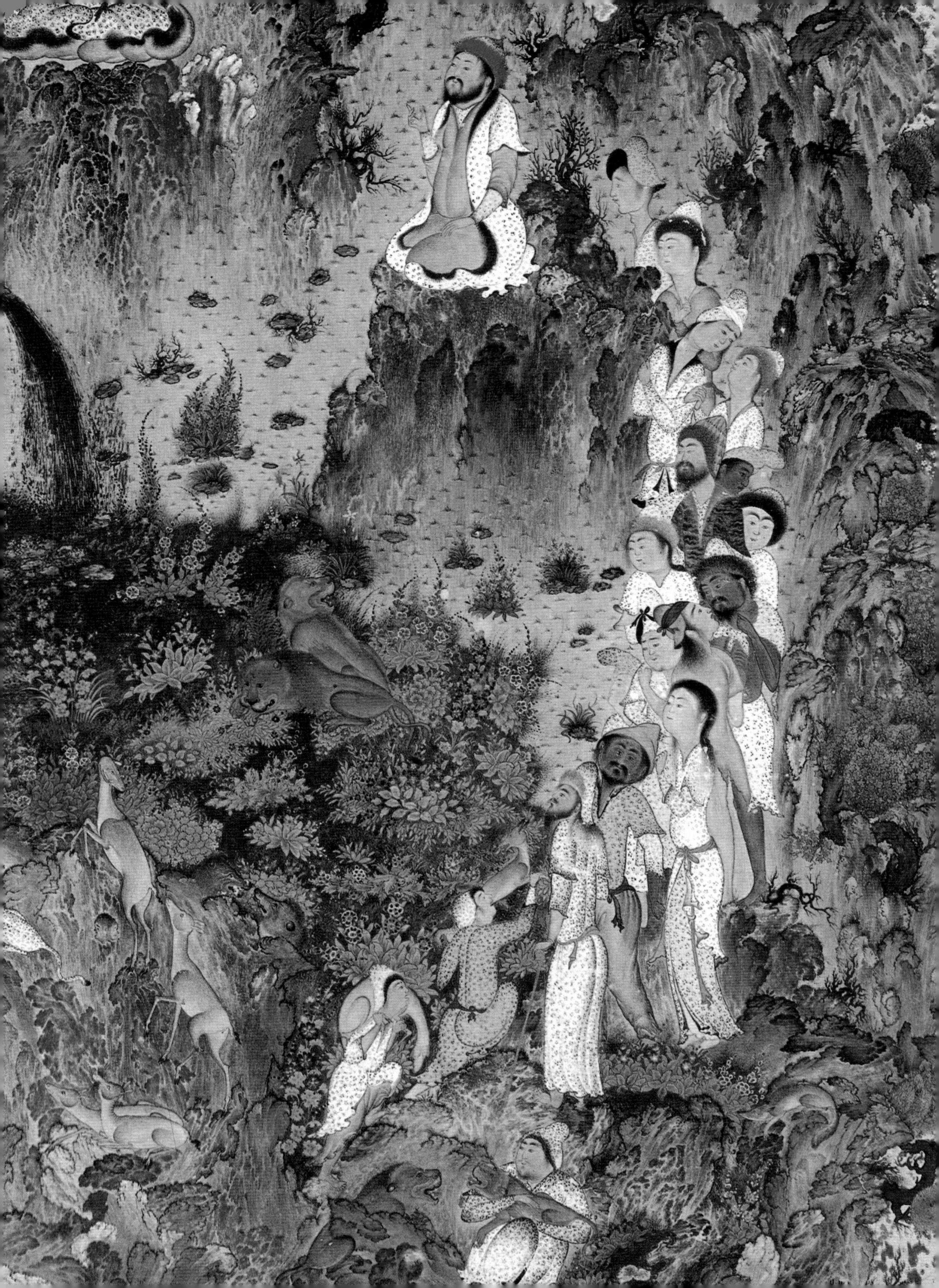

PLATE 4, folio 21 verso

Hushang Slays the Black Div

ATTRIBUTABLE TO SULTAN-MUHAMMAD

While Shah Gayumarth looked on with satisfaction (right), Siyamak's son Hushang avenged his father's death by killing the Black Div.

Whereas the incomparable *Court of Gayumarth* (Plate 2) was one of Sultan-Muhammad's most ambitious pictures and may have taken several years to complete, this stylistically similar miniature was dashingly sketched and painted, probably in a few days. It can be dated to about 1522, soon after the *Shah-nama* project began. Dazzling in its light-hearted wit, it must have delighted Prince Tahmasp, who was a precocious eight-year-old when it was painted for him.

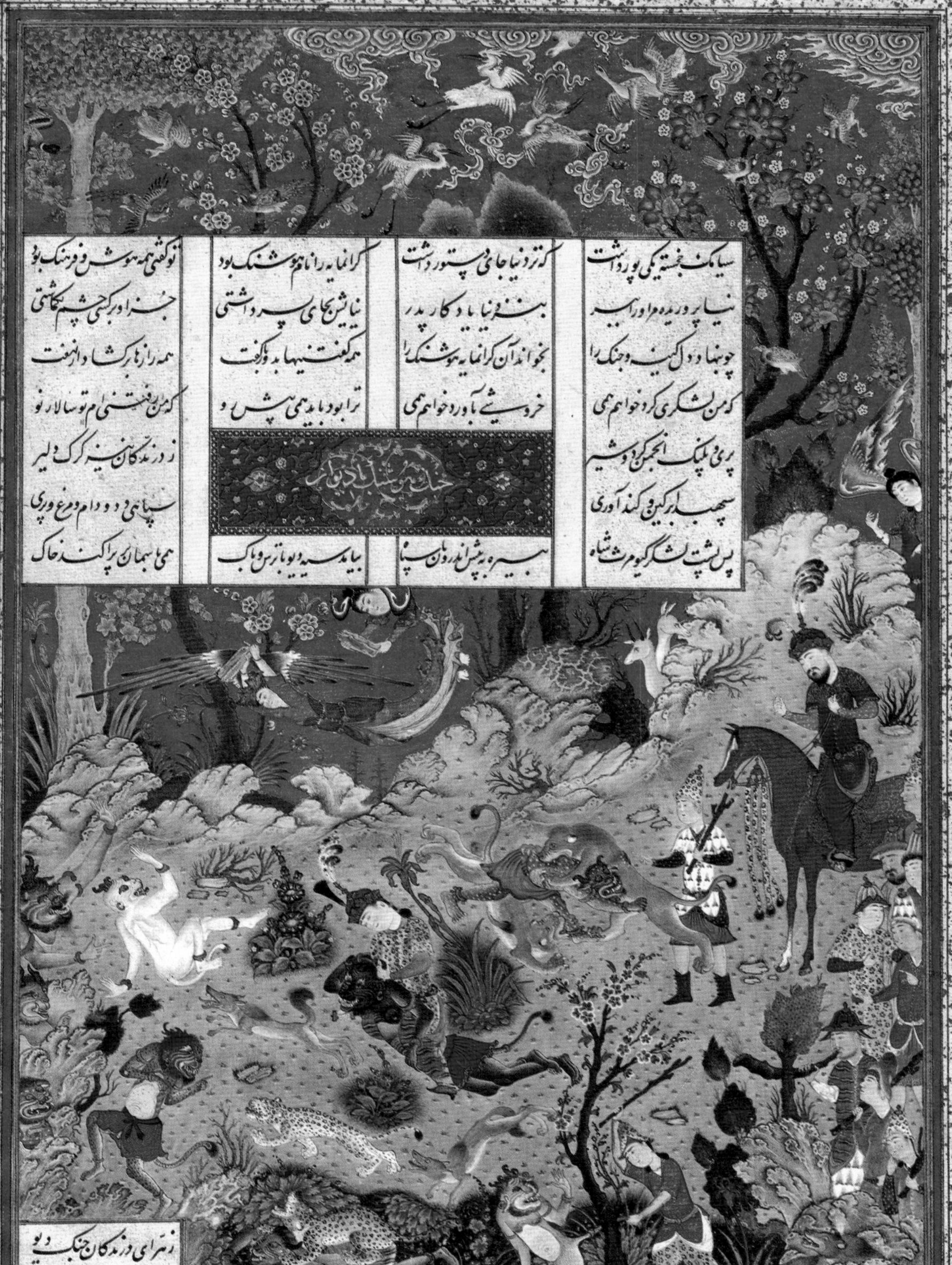
سیامک خجسته یکی پور داشت
که نزد نیا جاه دستور داشت
گرانمایه را نام هوشنگ بود
تو گفتی همه هوش و فرهنگ بود
نیا پروریده مر او را ببر
بنزد نیا یادگار پدر
نیایش بجای پسر داشتی
جز او بر کسی چشم نگماشتی
چو بنهاد دل کینه و جنگ را
بخواند آن گرانمایه هوشنگ را
همه گفتنیها بدو بازگفت
همه رازها برگشاد از نهفت
که من لشکری کرد خواهم همی
خروشی برآورد خواهم همی
ترا بود باید همی پیش رو
که من رفتنی‌ام تو سالار نو
جنگ هوشنگ با دیو
پری و پلنگ انجمن کرد و شیر
ز درندگان گرگ و ببر دلیر
سپهبد ابر کین و کندآوری
سپاهی دد و دام و مرغ و پری
پس پشت لشکر کیومرث شاه
نبیره به پیش اندرون با سپاه
بیامد سیه دیو با ترس و باک
همی به آسمان بر پراگند خاک
ز هرای درندگان جنگ دیو
شده سست وز خشم کیهان خدیو

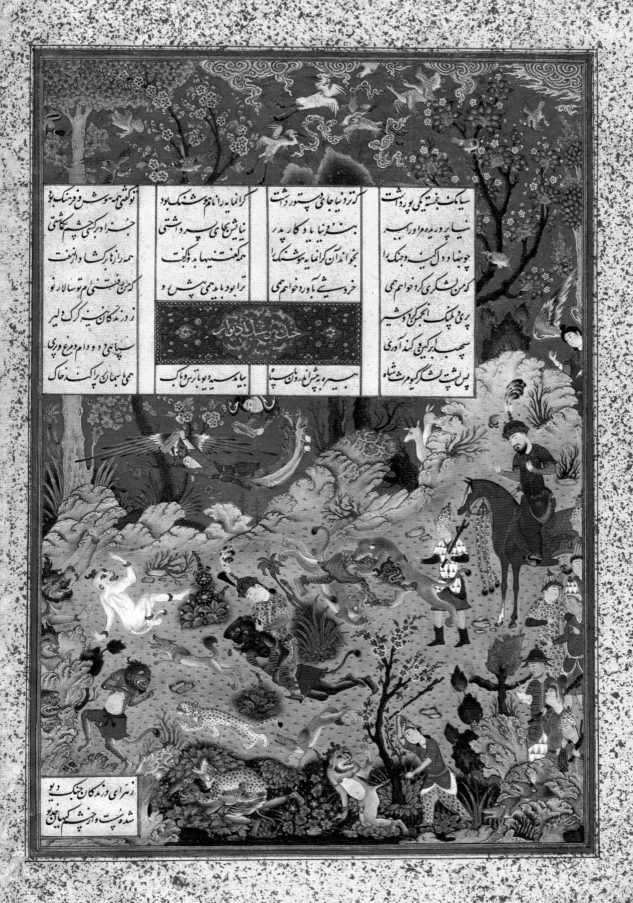

PLATE 5, folio 21 verso

Hushang Slays the Black Div/detail, *A Div threatens a leopard*

ATTRIBUTABLE TO SULTAN-MUHAMMAD

Hushang was assisted in his war against the forces of evil by an army of angels and animals whose loyalty went back to the blissful days of Gayumarth's reign from Iran's loftiest mountain (see Plates 2 and 3).

These zany but lively characterizations and expressively illogical spatial relationships are characteristic of Sultan-Muhammad, particularly during his early period.

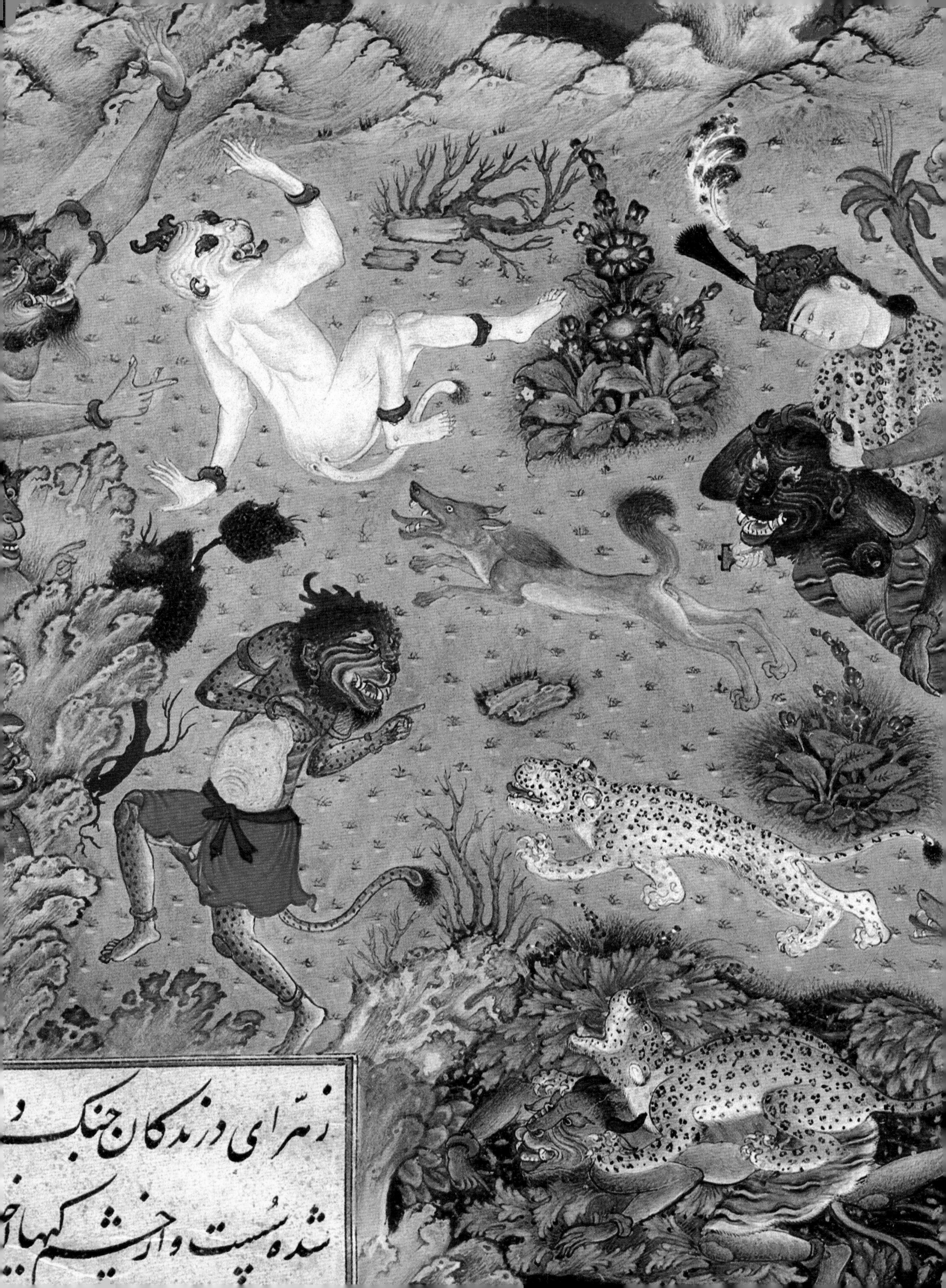
زهرّای درندکان جنگ
شده سُست و از خشم

PLATE 6, folio 37 verso

The Death of Zahhak

ATTRIBUTABLE TO SULTAN-MUHAMMAD

Zahhak, one of the villains of the *Shah-nama*, yielded as a young man to the temptation of evil Ahriman, who promised to kill his father and make him king. In return, Zahhak was afflicted with a pair of hungry snakes that grew from his shoulders. As their appetites could only be appeased by regular servings of human brains, Zahhak was compelled to sacrifice two youths to them daily. Such monstrous acts resulted in a revolt of his people, led by Faridun, who is shown here holding his bull-headed mace while the ill-fated tyrant is being chained to the summit of Mount Damavand "so that his brain might chafe and his agony endure."

This minutely finished and dramatic scene was painted by Sultan-Muhammad after the synthesis of his earlier, wilder manner with the subtler, more naturalistic idiom associated with the great Timurid master, Bihzad (see Introduction, page 17). It is probably his last important work for the *Shah-nama* and is already in the style associated with his next major project, the *Khamsa* of Nizami (see Plates 19–33).

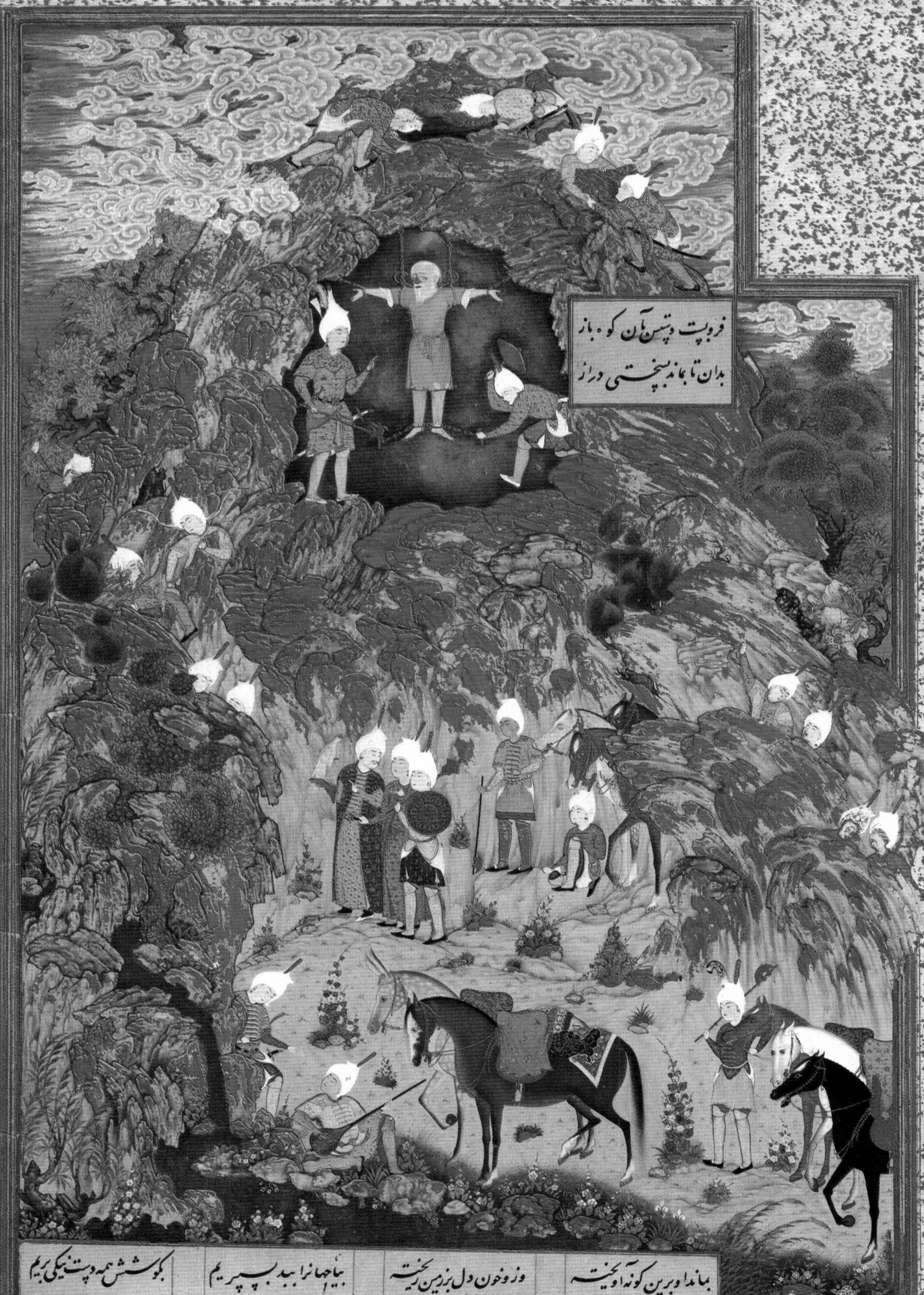

فروبست دستش بر آن کوه باز
بدان تا بماند بسختی دراز
بماند او برین گونه آویخته
وزو خون دل بر زمین ریخته
نباشد همی نیک و بد پایدار
همان به که نیکی بود یادگار
بیا تا جهان را ببد نسپریم
بکوشش همه دست نیکی بریم
سخن ماند از تو همی یادگار
سخن را چنین خوار مایه مدار

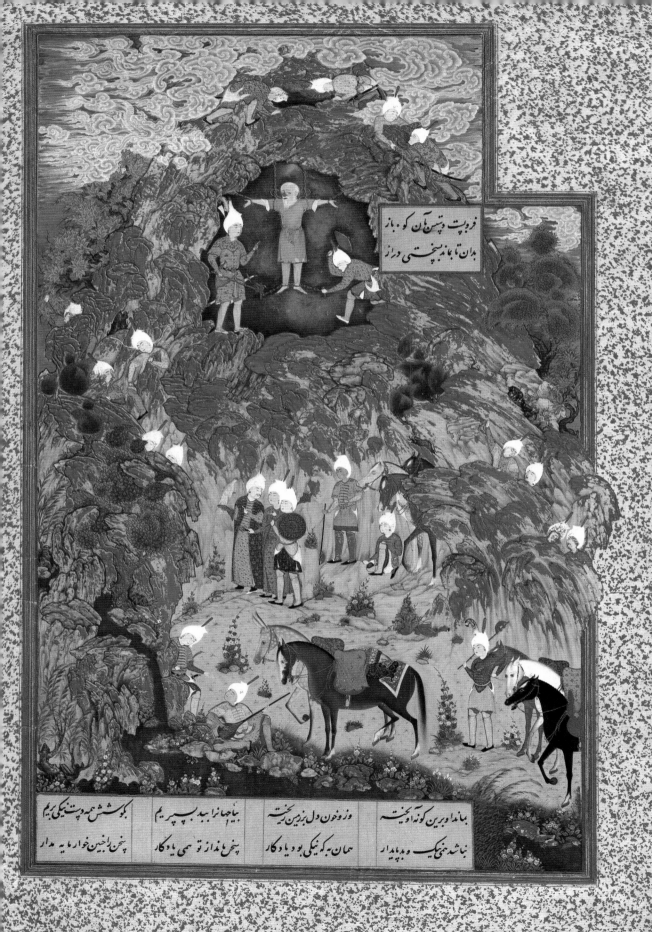

PLATE 7, folio 37 verso

The Death of Zahhak/detail, *Courtiers, musicians, a horse, and a mule*

ATTRIBUTABLE TO SULTAN-MUHAMMAD

In contrast to the painful fate of King Zahhak, the foreground of this miniature, with its elegant figures and animals, evokes a royal picnic.

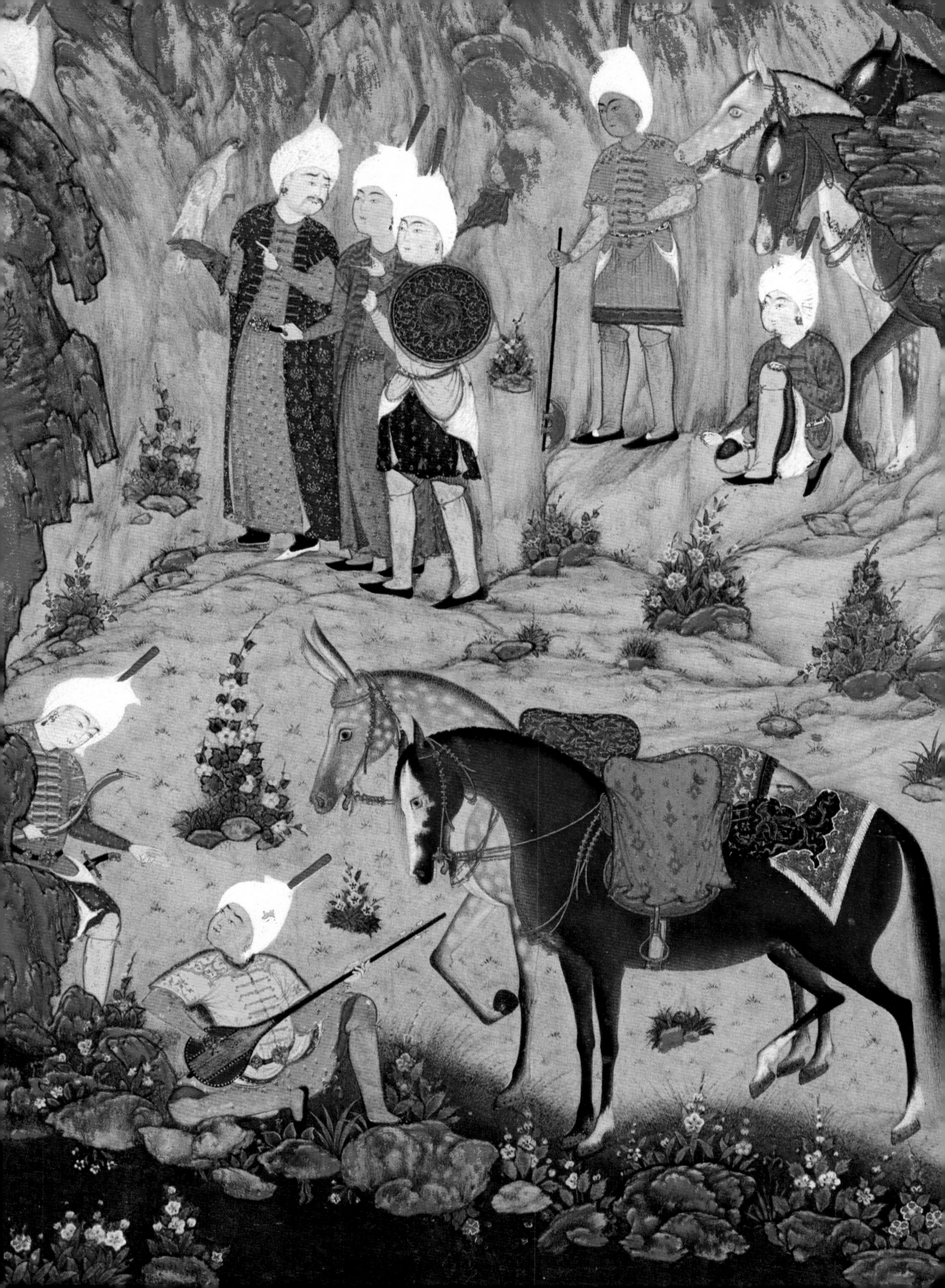

PLATE 8, folio 62 verso

Zal Is Sighted by a Caravan

ATTRIBUTABLE TO PAINTER D (ABD-AL AZIZ?)

Although perfectly formed in every other respect, Sam's son Zal was born with hair white as snow, a bad omen. Bitterly disappointed, Sam exposed the infant to die near a distant mountain. But Zal did not die. He was adopted by a monstrous bird, the simurgh (phoenix), who brought him up with her own young in a mountain aerie. Years later, a caravan of merchants sighted the white-haired youth in the great bird's nest. When Sam, having grown to regret his earlier cruel decision, heard the news, he hastened to his son's rescue. A sad parting then took place between the frosty-haired prince and his feathered foster mother, who gave him some plumes to burn as a signal if ever he needed her help. Then Zal returned to "civilization." In time he became Shah of Iran and sired Rustam, the *Shah-nama*'s most renowned hero.

This brilliantly colored miniature is the work of an unidentified member of the royal atelier (possibly Abd-al Aziz), tentatively dubbed by us Painter D. His Tabriz-oriented style is strongly reminiscent of the late fifteenth-century Turkman drawing reproduced above (Figure 1, page 15). For other examples of this artist's work, painted in the style of ca. 1560, see Plate 43, Figures o, p, s, and t.

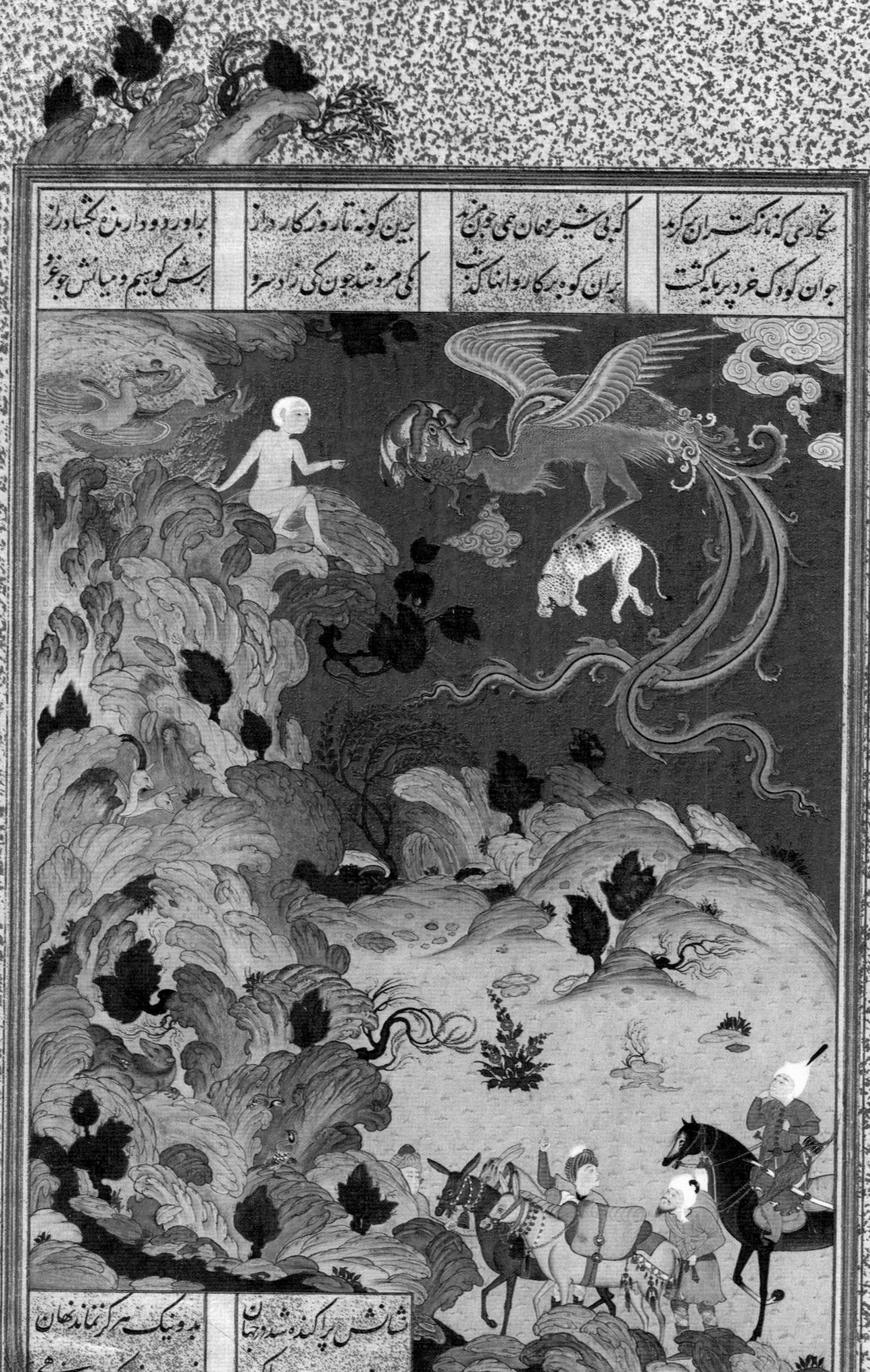
جوان کودک خرد پرمایه گشت
بران کوه بر کاروانها گذشت
بدین گونه تا روزگاری دراز
یکی مرد شد چون یکی زاد سرو
برش کوه سیم و میانش چو غرو
نشانش پراگنده شد در جهان
بد و نیک هرگز نماند نهان
بسام نریمان رسید آگهی
ازان نیک پی پور با فرهی

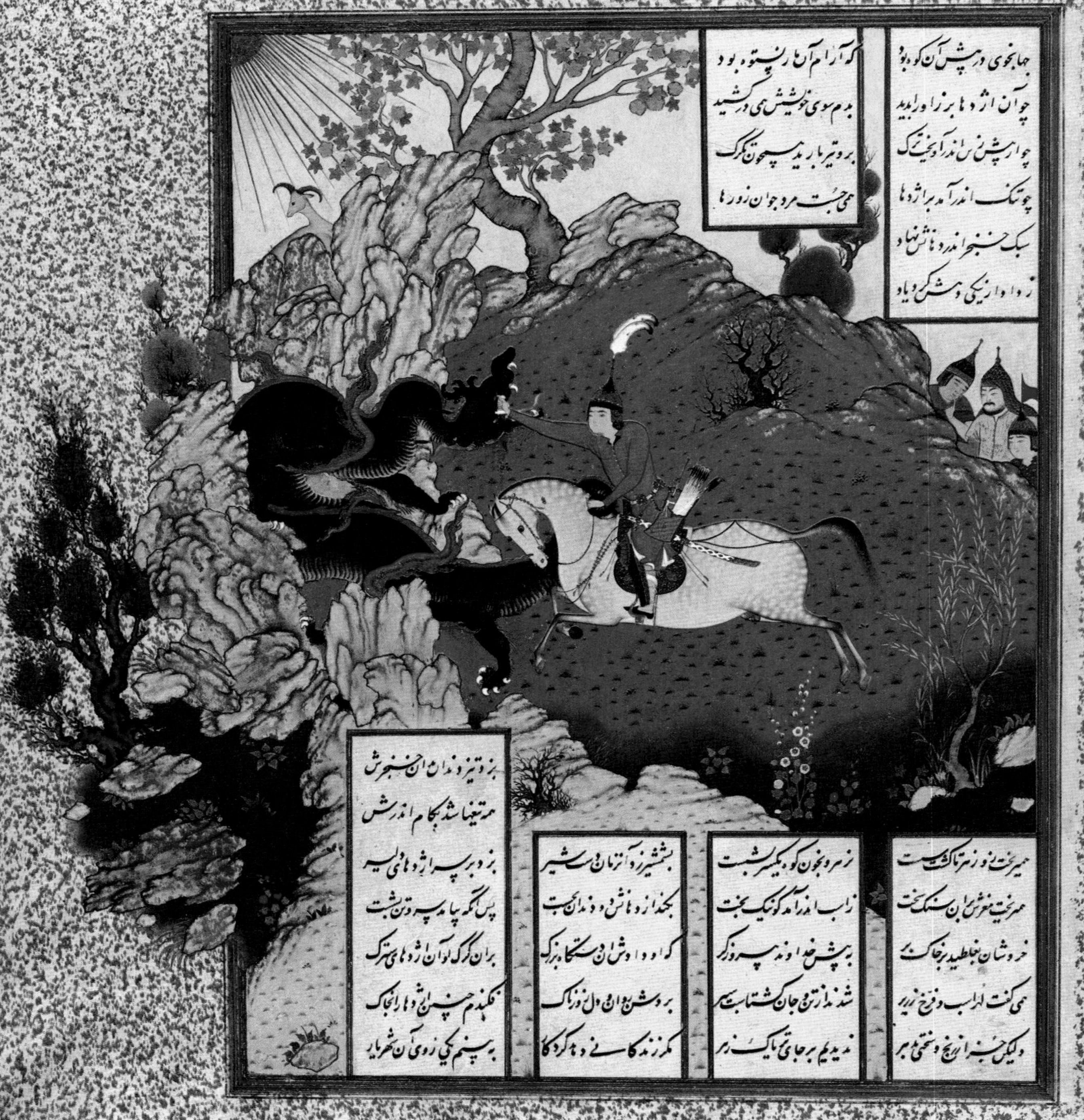

PLATE 9, folio 402 recto

Gushtasp Slays the Dragon of Mount Saqila

ATTRIBUTABLE TO MIRZA 'ALI

Gushtasp was the ill-appreciated son of Shah Luhrasp, from whose court he departed for Rum (Turkey) to make his fortune. While there, he fell in love with the emperor's daughter, whose hand he earned by carrying out a series of trials set by his would-be father-in-law. One of the mightiest huntsmen and warriors in the *Shah-nama*, he later slew the terrible dragon of Mount Saqila to help a friend who wanted to marry another of the emperor's daughters.

This sunlit picture can be recognized stylistically as an early work by Sultan-Muhammad's son Mirza 'Ali, one of the most talented second generation Safavid artists. Other miniatures by him are reproduced in Plates 10, 24, 26 and 27, 34 and 35, 36 and 37, 42, 44, and Figures i, and u.

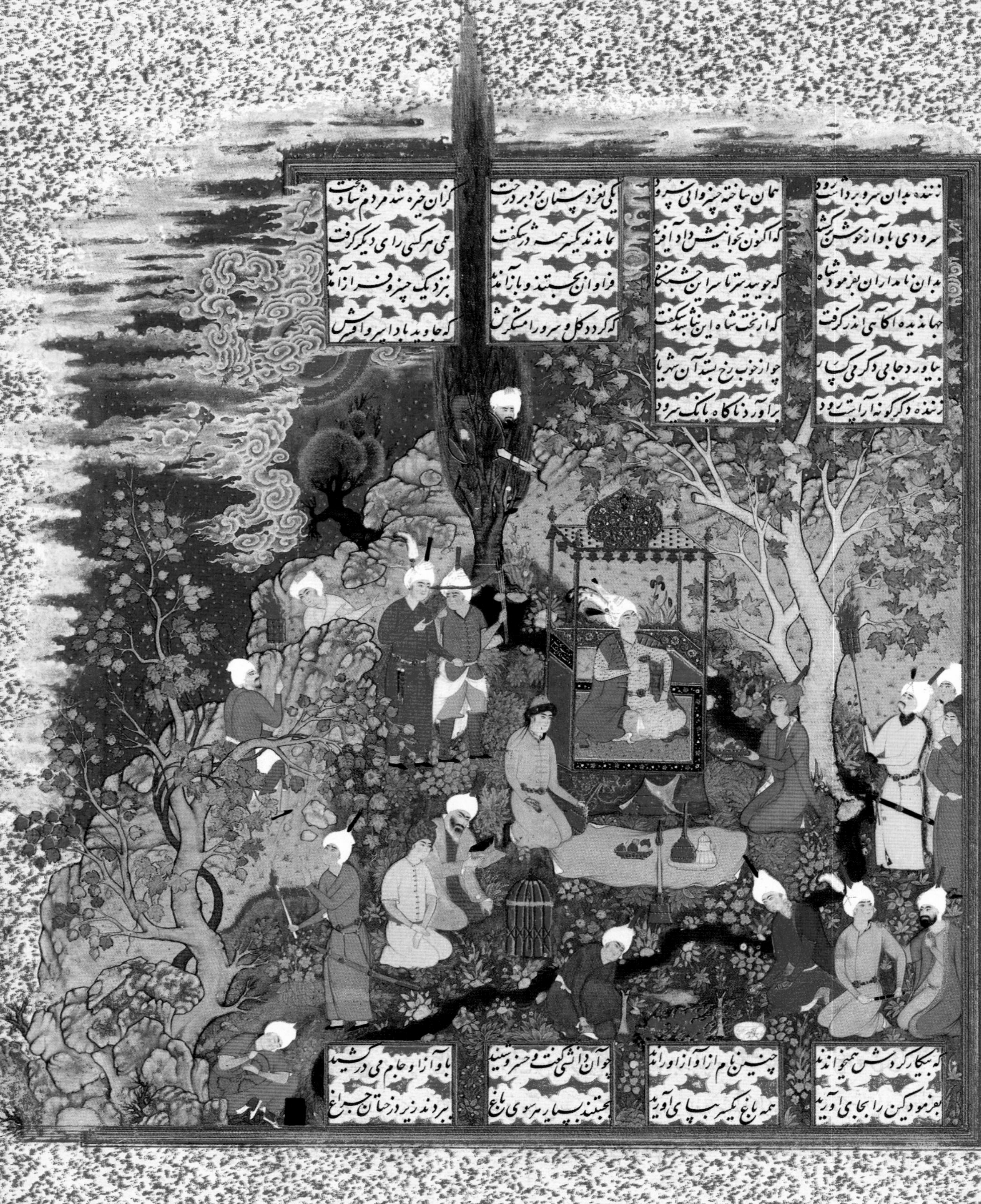
زننده بدان سرو برداشت رود
سرودی باواز خوش برکشید
بدان نامداران بفرمود شاه
جهاندیده آگاهی اندر گرفت
بیاورد جامی دگر می بکف
زننده دگرگونه آراست رود
همان ساخته پهلوانی سرود
که اکنون بخوانیش داد آفرید
که جویید سرتاسر این جشنگاه
که از بخت شاه این نباشد شگفت
چو از خوب رخ بستد آن شهریار
برآورد ناگاه بانگ سرود
یکی نغز دستان بزد بر درخت
بماندند یکسر همه در شگفت
فراوان بجستند و بازآمدند
که گردد گل و سرو رامشگرش
گران خیره شد مردم شادبخت
همی هر کسی رای دیگر گرفت
بنزدیک خسرو فراز آمدند
که جاوید بادا سر و افسرش
که بیکار گردش همی خواندند
بفرمود کین را بجای آورید
چنین نام از آواز او راندند
همه باغ یکسر بپای آورید
چو آن داستانی گفت و خسرو شنید
بجستند بسیار هر سوی باغ
با آواز او جام می درکشید
بردند زیر درختان چراغ

PLATE 10, folio 731 recto

Barbad, the Concealed Musician

ATTRIBUTABLE TO MIRZA 'ALI

The enterprising and gifted musician Barbad was nevertheless unknown at the court of Shah Khusraw Parviz, because Sarkad, the Shah's leading singer, had successfully prevented the auditions of fresh talent. After befriending a royal gardener, Barbad arranged to hide in the branches of a tree beneath which the Shah was expected to picnic. When Khusraw and his entourage had arrived and settled down to a pleasurable repast, Barbad burst into song, to the delight of the Shah and the consternation of Sarkad, who promptly told his royal patron that what he heard was not man-made music but a tribute to him from the wind. Soon, however, the superb concert continued. The excited Shah ordered his attendants to beat the bushes for the singer so that he could reward him by stuffing his mouth with precious stones and pearls. Upon hearing this, Barbad slipped down from his perch. Happily, he did not choke on his reward; and he was appointed court musician in place of nasty Sarkad (see also Plates, 26, 27).

Although this miniature was painted when Mirza 'Ali was very young, it is already characteristic in revealing the artist's concern for psychological nuances, his intricate study of still life, and his mastery of rhythmic but architectonic composition.

کوندوز آتشام غمچه باغی چاک چاک
چونکه حسدین اوتتی رنج و درد انکا
کافر ظالم سرشت عشوه گر
یانه اول منظردین اولدی جلوه گر

کیچه تانک آتغونچه فرقتدین هلاک
تو فراغ اولدی جسم غم پرورد انکا

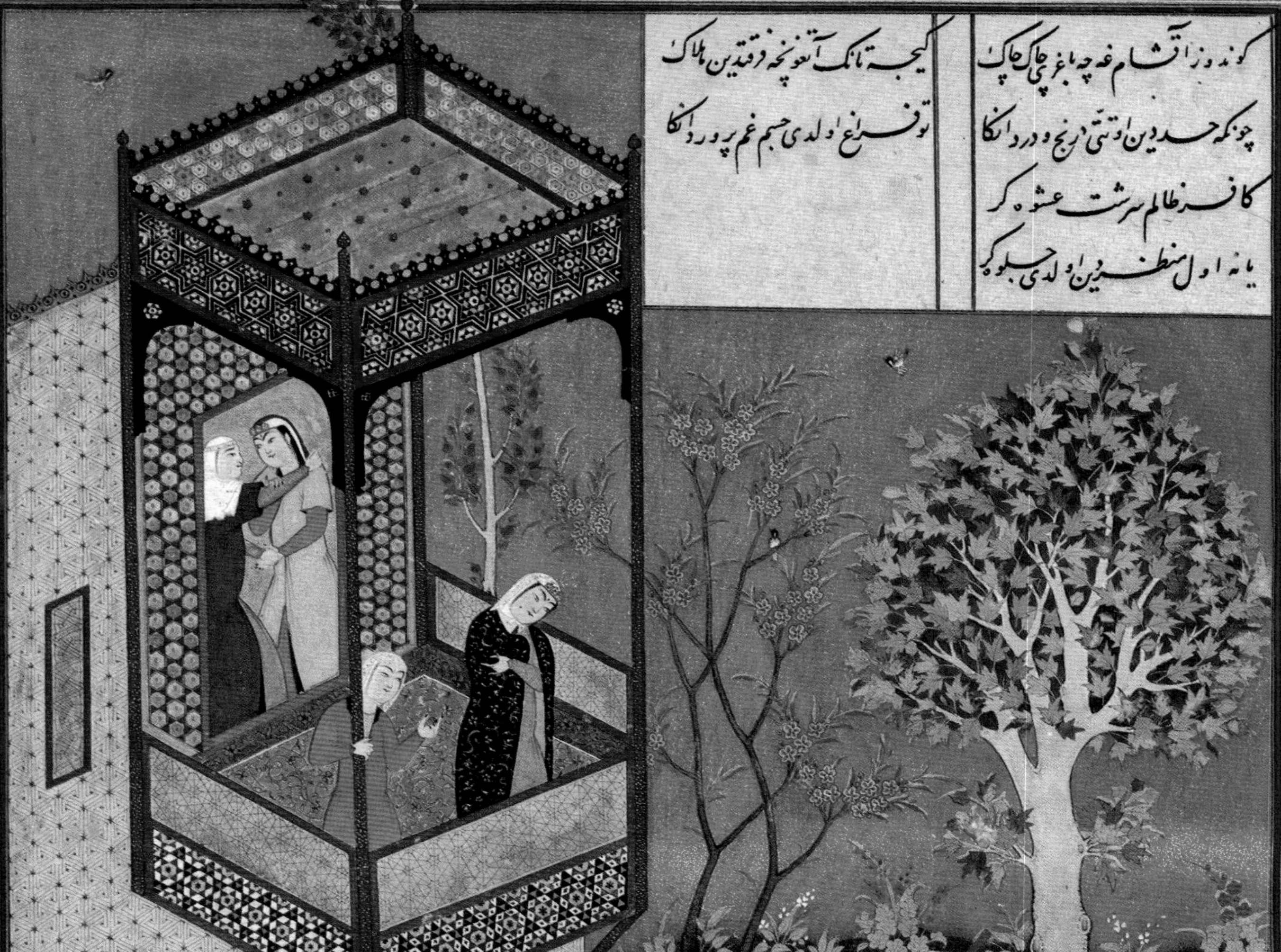

اوت سالیب عالم غه حسن و نازیدین
چون سنکا کعبه طوافی ایردی فن
منزل ایدا پیر کیچه اهل سفر

سوزی اوز افتاده سی تنک رازیدین
دیر ایشیکیندا یندین توتونک وطن
توتسا تیکین تانکلاسی ایلار گذر

کیم ایا اسلام ایلیکا راهبر
سینی دیرلار دین ایلیکا دستگیر
سنچ کیم پیر آی سکون فن ایلامیش

دین و اسلام اهلیغه ارشاد گر
کفر دیریغه سیدین بولدونک اسیر
دیر تو فراغینی مسکن ایلامیش

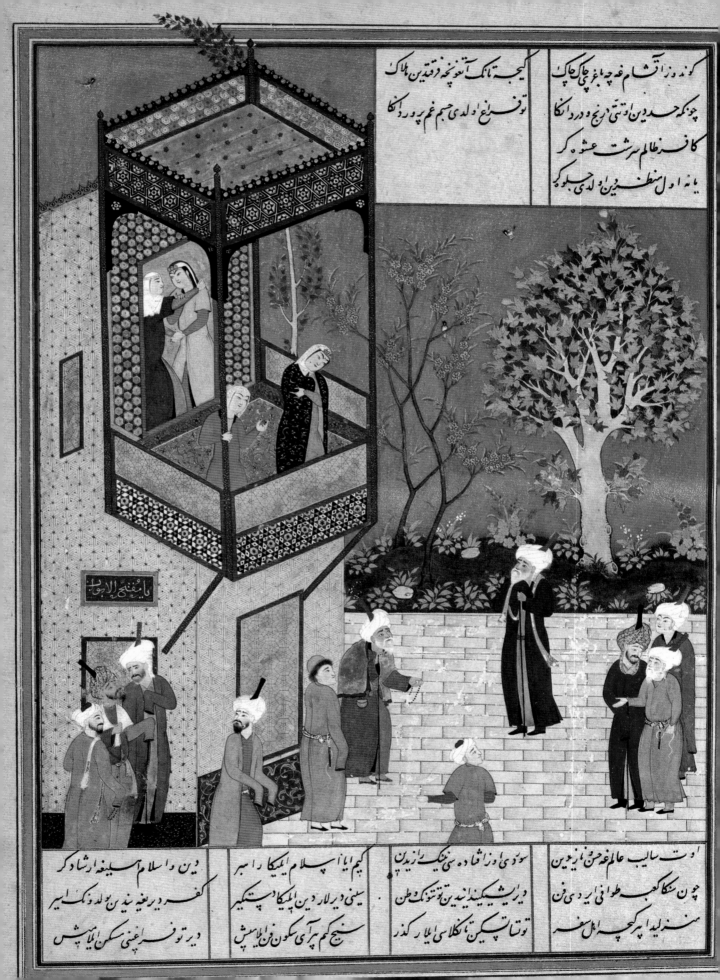

Collected Works of Mir 'Ali Shir Nawa'i

PLATE 11, folio 169 recto

The Crazed Old Shaykh of San'an

ATTRIBUTABLE TO SHAYKH ZADEH

After seeing a beautiful Christian girl in his dreams, the pious Shaykh of San'an persuaded his fellow holy men to travel to Rum to search for her. Amazingly, he succeeded; and here is shown horrifying his colleagues by renouncing Islam to win her affections.

On grounds of style, this picture can be ascribed to the Herat-trained artist, Shaykh Zadeh, who typically has underdramatized the subject. Instead of focusing on the people, he concentrated on the formal arrangement of color areas, elaborated passages of geometric and arabesque ornament, and symbolized the girl and her impassioned lover as a pair of trees, one youthful and delicate, the other past maturity and massive. (For other works by Shaykh Zadeh, see Plates 12, 14, and 16.)

بولوب ایردوک حصولی ایچره عاجز
ایلشینک عذریدا یوز پیر دیک اوتانغانی
قولوب عذر اول طبق باشینی آچتی
تیغیب چینی انفاسی شتابی
دیدی جان پرورانغا پیسیکدین اولدوم
مینی غربت ارا بیچاره ایتکان
انینکدیک آه طوفانین چیقاردی
ہمول ایردی که مفتون بولمیش ایردی
پراوکیم بولسامی نینک ذکریدین مست

منز ایرماس قولونک کورکوزدی معجز
نی پیردین تیکزیدین الیکنغه یانغای
جواهرنی انینک باشیغه سا چتی
تیشیب کوکسینی کونکلی اضطرابی
اونونکدین عمر رخیدین قوتولدوم
دیار و ملک دین آواره ایتکان
که مهوشنینک نقابی بیلکا باردی
کوروب کوزکو دا مجنون بولمیش ایردی
نی تاتنک ایکاندا بولسا یر اوزره پست

اکر یوز قرن عذر آیین بولالی
تیلاتتی پر طبق پیرله جواهر
پری وش نو فصاحت پیرله مفتون
تنی تیز اتما دین آرام تاپمای
نی انکلای کیم قایومه روا کین سین
چیقیب جانیم اونونکدین بولغاچ آکاه
کورونکاج اول جمال عالم آرا
پراوکیم عکس کورکاج هوشی کیتیب

نیتیب پرکونچی لیک عذرونک قولالی
دیدی فرزدنک ایماس ای شیتامام
اوزیدین بیخبر فرها د مجنون
بوبلی آرام لیق انجام تاپمای
الچیم قان ایلاکان سین مو اکین سین
یوزونکنی کورمای اولدوم آه دیوز آه
انینک مطلوبی بولدی آشکارا
اوزین کورکاچ نی تانک جانی کیتیبا
چو فرها دا اول پری ایرکانینی بیلدی
چیکیب اوتلوق فغان اندا اسقلدی

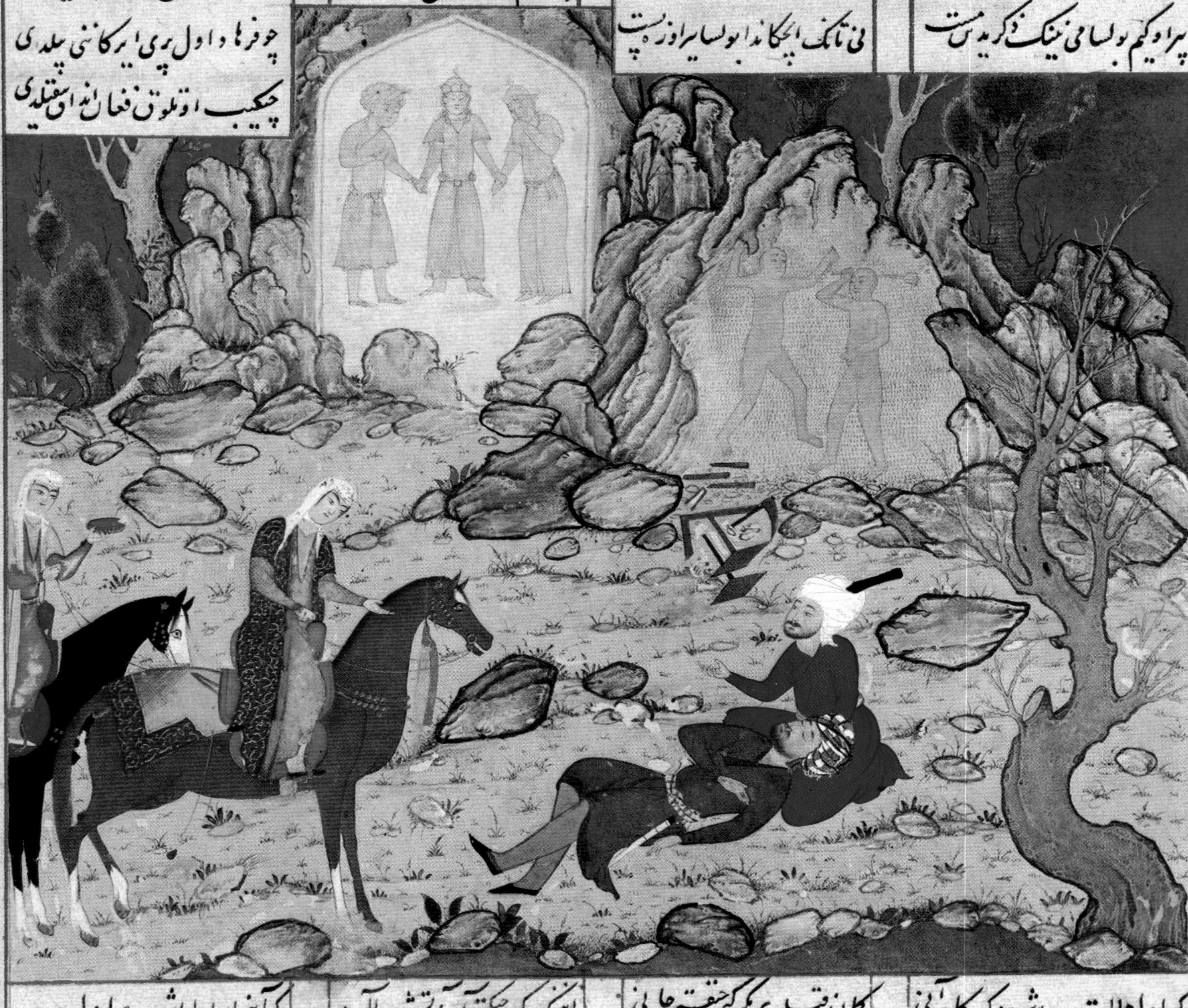

کیم اول حالت دا شیرین کورکاچ آنی
چراول شمع وفاداقالمادی نور

کان قیلدی کیم کیم حقیقی جانی
بیتیب پروانه دیک باشیغه شاپور

اینکدیک چیکتی آه آتش آلود
باشیدین قوبی غه آدی یغلابان زار

که آنی ابرار باشوردی اول دود
که ای یوق قیمتینک جز رنج و آزار

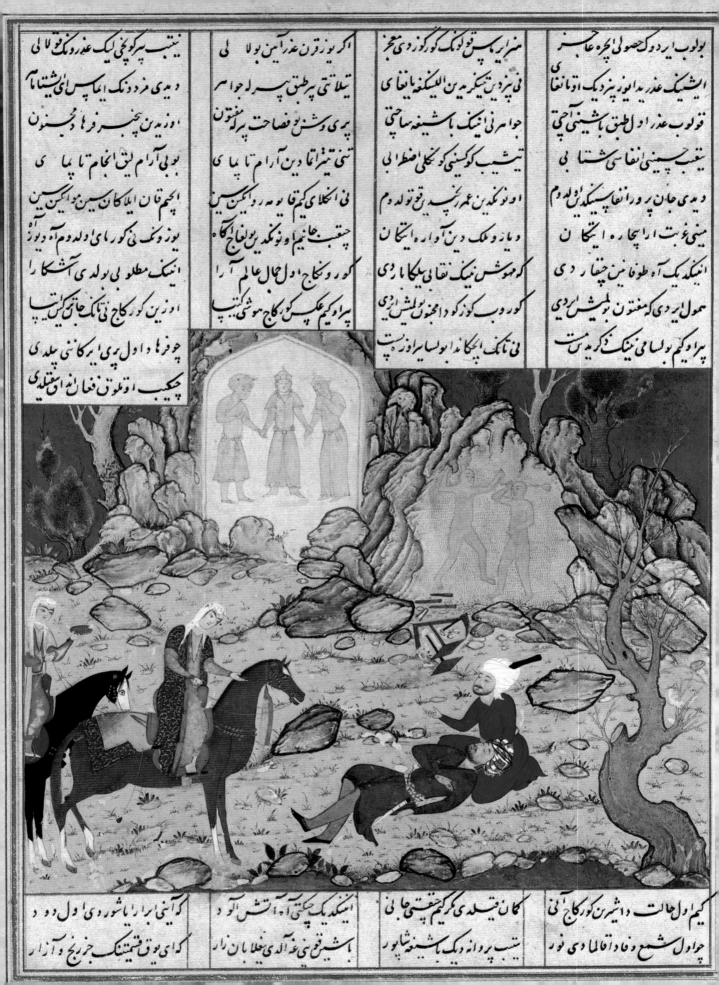

PLATE 12, folio 268 recto

Shirin Discovers the Corpse of Farhad

ATTRIBUTABLE TO SHAYKH ZADEH

Although the Armenian Princess Shirin's lover was Shah Khusraw (see Plates 24, 25, 26, 27), she was also beloved by Farhad, an ingenious young sculptor-engineer who befriended her before ever meeting her by building a conduit to bring the milk she craved to her castle. When she thanked him in person for his help, he fell passionately in love with her, thereby arousing Khusraw's jealousy. The Shah ordered the young man brought to him and tried to appease his ardor by offering bribes and threats. When this failed, he promised him Shirin's hand if Farhad would cut a road through Mount Bisitun, a task considered impossible.

Farhad began by carving an image of his beloved Shirin (though the sculptures in the picture appear to have been inspired by rock-cut reliefs of the Sassanian period), after which he hacked away at his apparently endless tunnel. Although she did not return Farhad's love, Shirin was so moved by his devotion that she visited him as he labored. At the sight of her, the sculptor fainted; and when news of this reached the Shah his jealousy was further inflamed. Khusraw conceived a plot: an old crone would tell Farhad that Shirin was dead. When he heard the "news," Farhad was so horrified that he hurled himself from a cliff and was killed. Shirin came at once and mourned over his corpse. Later, she ordered that a dome be built over his grave, a monument to true lovers.

PLATE 13, folio 350 verso

Bahram Gur Hunting before Azada

ATTRIBUTABLE TO SULTAN-MUHAMMAD

When Bahram Gur, son of Shah Yazdgird the Sinner, was born, his father agreed to send him to Yemen in Arabia to be educated under the tutelage of wise Monzer. There he grew and learned, mastering the arts of letters, polo, hunting, horsemanship, and warfare. At eighteen, considering his training complete, the Prince dismissed his instructors, after presenting them with generous gifts. Now, he decided, it was time to fulfill his life through women. Monzer notified a slave dealer, who brought forty Greek slave girls for him to choose from. Bahram selected two. One was Azada, who played the lyre, the other a tulip-cheeked lass as beautiful as Canopus. Here, the two girls look on while Bahram glories in his horsemanship and dispatches a wild ass.

Sultan-Muhammad treated Bahram's pleasures with his usual wit and profundity, stressing the cruelty as well as joy of nature. Stylistically, this miniature is extremely close to the master's only signed pictures, in the *Diwan* of Hafiz (Plates 17, 18).

کاه بستان دلکشا اچره　　قصر و ایوان جانفزا اچره　　شه توزوب بزم اول پری پرلا　　چرخ خورشید خاوری پ

اول نوا چکپا بو فغان تاریب　　اول چو زخسار آچیب بوجان تاریب　　کاه صحرا نورد و دشت خرام　　ایچباس صیدنینک نشاطی غه جا

اندا هم بحرین اتفاق ایتمای　　آینی اوزدین دمی ییراق ایتمای　　اصلی دا اول غزاله مشکین　　چین قضا سیدا ایردی حجله نشیر

هم حسن دشتی و امقام ایتکان　　هم کل و سبزه دا خرام ایتکان　　دشت اوزره غزال مشکین بو　　لاله و سبزه اوزره قیلغان خو

چون انکا بو صفت شمایل ایدی　　دشت سیر یغه اسرو مایل ایدی　　شه غه خود دشت ساری ایش چاپماق　　صید قیلماق بیله فرح تاپماق

ایکیسی طبعیغه ملایم پسیر　　بو جهت بدین الارغه دایم پسیر　　سیر اراشغه صید ایدی آیین　　همرهی ماه روی مهد نشین

نچه کیم شاه صید اتیار ایردی

شه نی اول ماصید اتیار ایردی

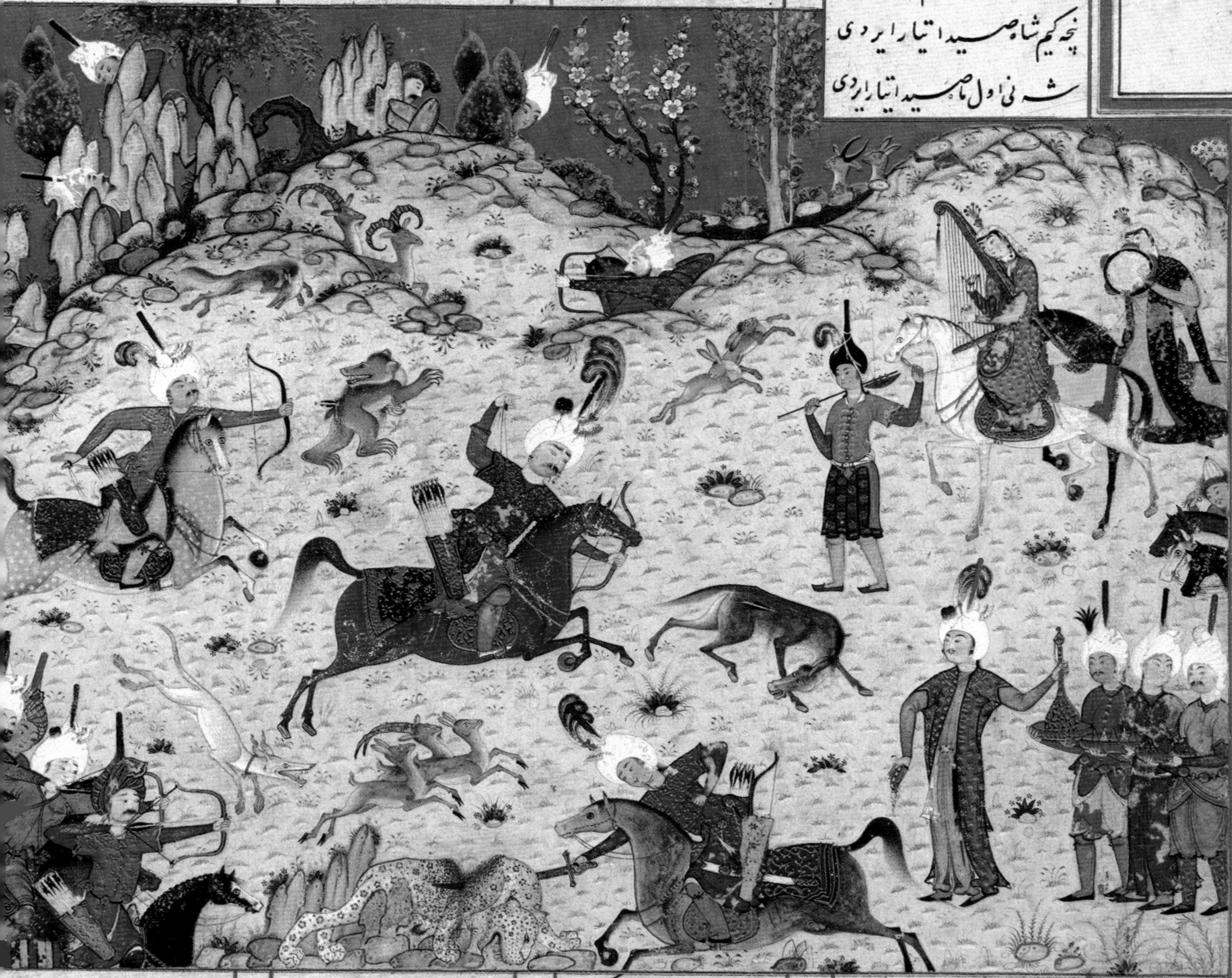

قایسی پر صید کیم شه ایتسا هلاک　　نغمه تارتیب اول بت چالاک　　شور و غوغا جهان غه سالور ایدی　　بل شه کامران غه سالور اید

شوق اوتی اچره شاه ازاد　　مهوشیدن تیلار ایدی باده　　که اوتین بو سوپیر له یپت ایتکای　　شعله اول سو بیله نشست ایتکا

می بولور ایردی خود شرار انگیز　　شوقی نینک شعله سی قیلور ایدی تیز　　نغمه دین اوتی دم تاپار ایردی　　باده دین یاغ هم تاپار ایرد

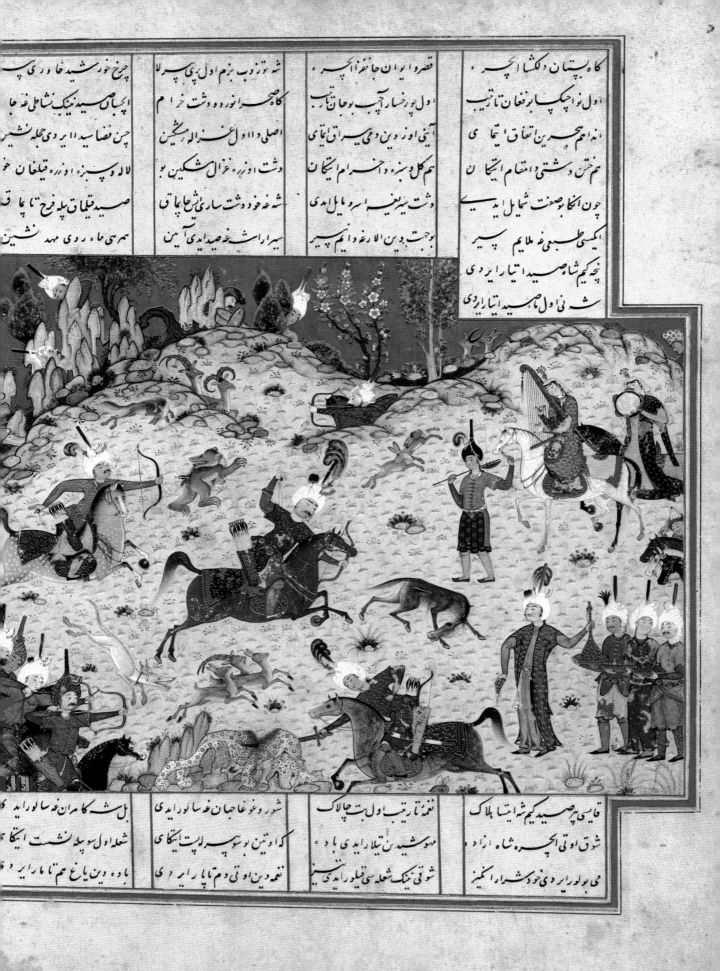

PLATE 14, folio 415 verso

Iskandar (Alexander the Great) in Battle against Darius

ATTRIBUTABLE TO SHAYKH ZADEH

In Iranian literature, Alexander the Great (Iskandar) was seen as a noble, sympathetic conqueror, well-versed in philosophy. His chivalry was underscored in the tale of his defeat of the Achaemenid emperor, Darius (or Dara). After the rout of his army, shown here, Darius was mortally stabbed by two of his own men to curry favor with Alexander, who, however, went to the dying emperor, promised to restore him to health and power, and ordered the traitors hanged. Sadly, Darius expired anyway.

Shaykh Zadeh's buoyant composition glorifies battle as a formal ballet on horseback.

آلارغه که شاه خسرو رهنمون
چو بارتی توکلتی کلامین تمام
آتی نعلیدین تاکه خود دیدا اسپل
فلک سیری آشوب سوست ایله
آنی رزم ایلی شیر دران دپیان

عنایت قیلیب اردی میندین فزون
الار دین کیم اول ایلامیش اردی کام
کریب کوک تیمور ایچره انداق کیپل
ساچیب پل دماغیغه فرست ایله
آتین انجمن اهلی خسران دپیان
توکا تکاج دعا چاپتی بارق قه تیز

بولورکیم پیاپی روان ایلاکای
روان بولدی سیدانغه قاتل وشی
آتی تغلیدین کیم شرار ایرلیب
حمایل داغی تیغی سجاده دیک
چو میدان طریقین ادا ایلادی
انکا داغی بارق بولوب برق خیز

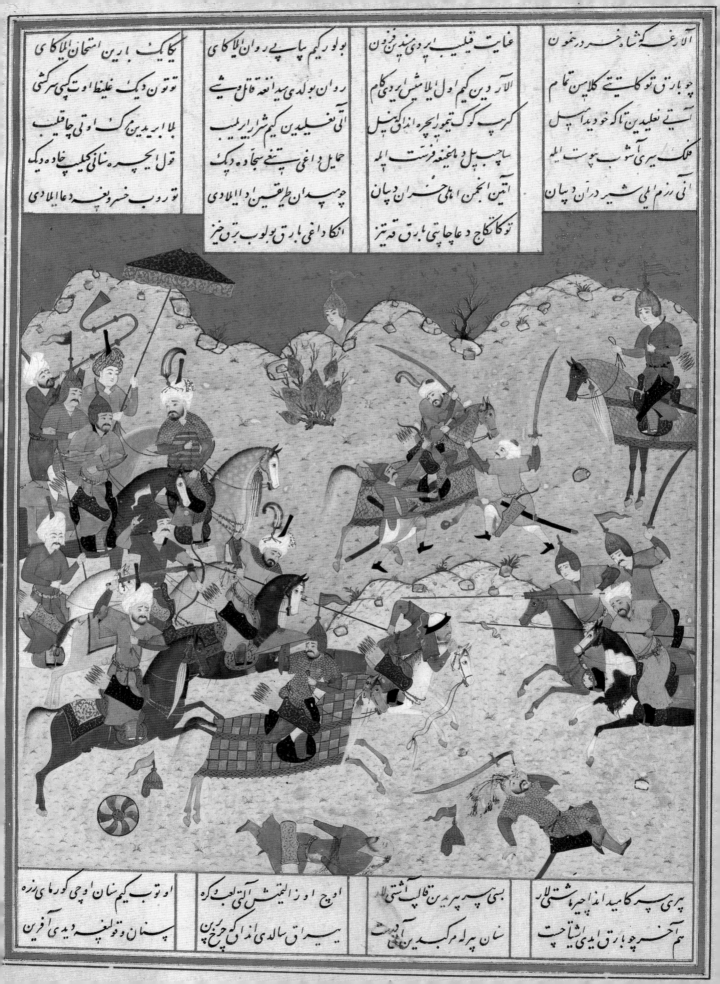

یکایک بارین امتحان ایلاکای
توتون دیک غلیظ اوت کپی سرکشی
بلا ابر یدین مرک اوتی چاقلیب
قول ایچره سنانی کلیب خاده دیک
توروب خسرو یغه دعا ایلادی

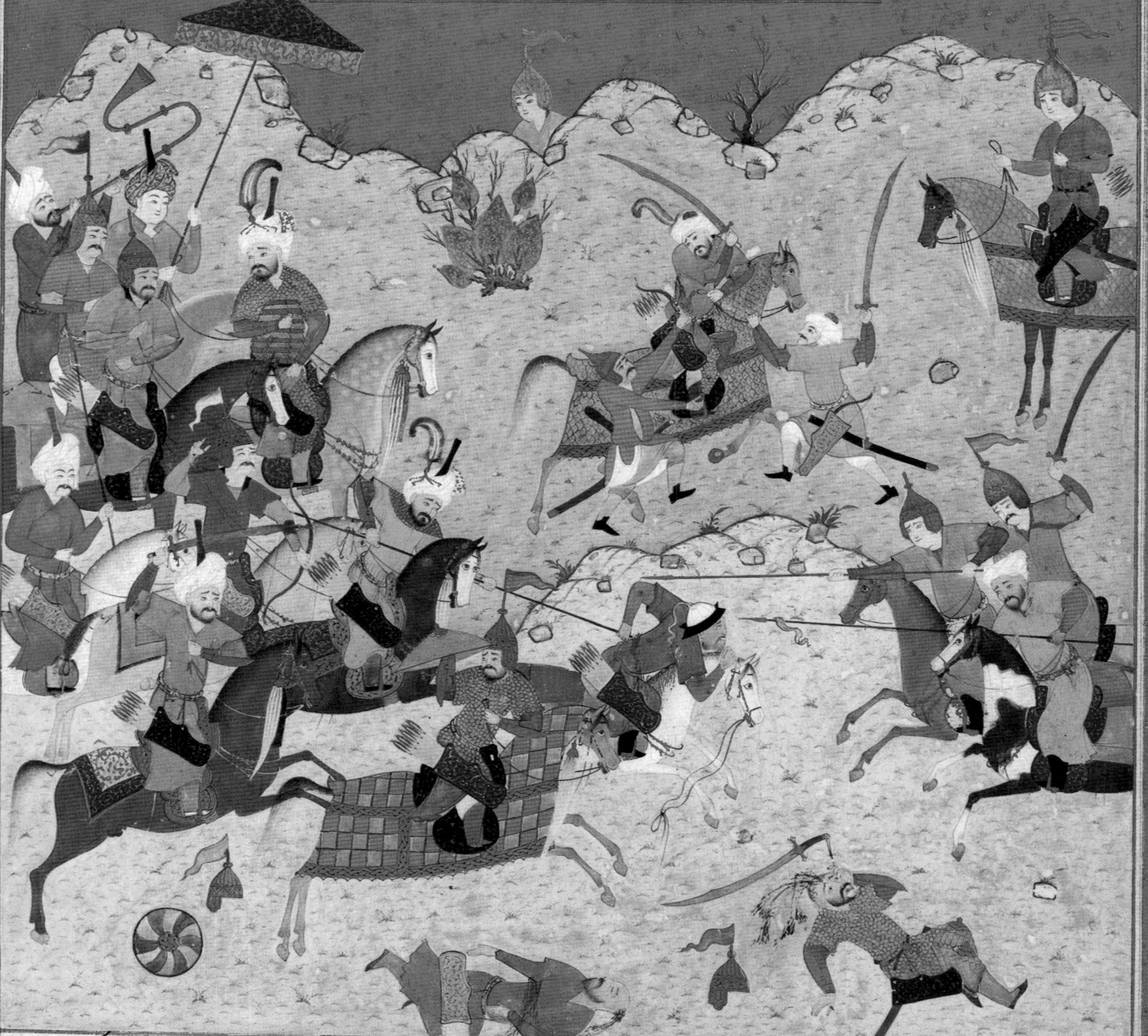

پری سپر کامید انداچیرماشتی لار
هم آخر چو بارتی ایدی اشیا جیت

بسی سپر سپر یدین قالیب آشتی لار
سنان پیرله مرکبدین آتتی دست

اوچ اوز الیمتش آلتی لعب وکره
سیراق سالدی انداق که چرخ برین

او توب کیم سنان اوچی کورمای زره
سنان و قولغه دیدی آفرین

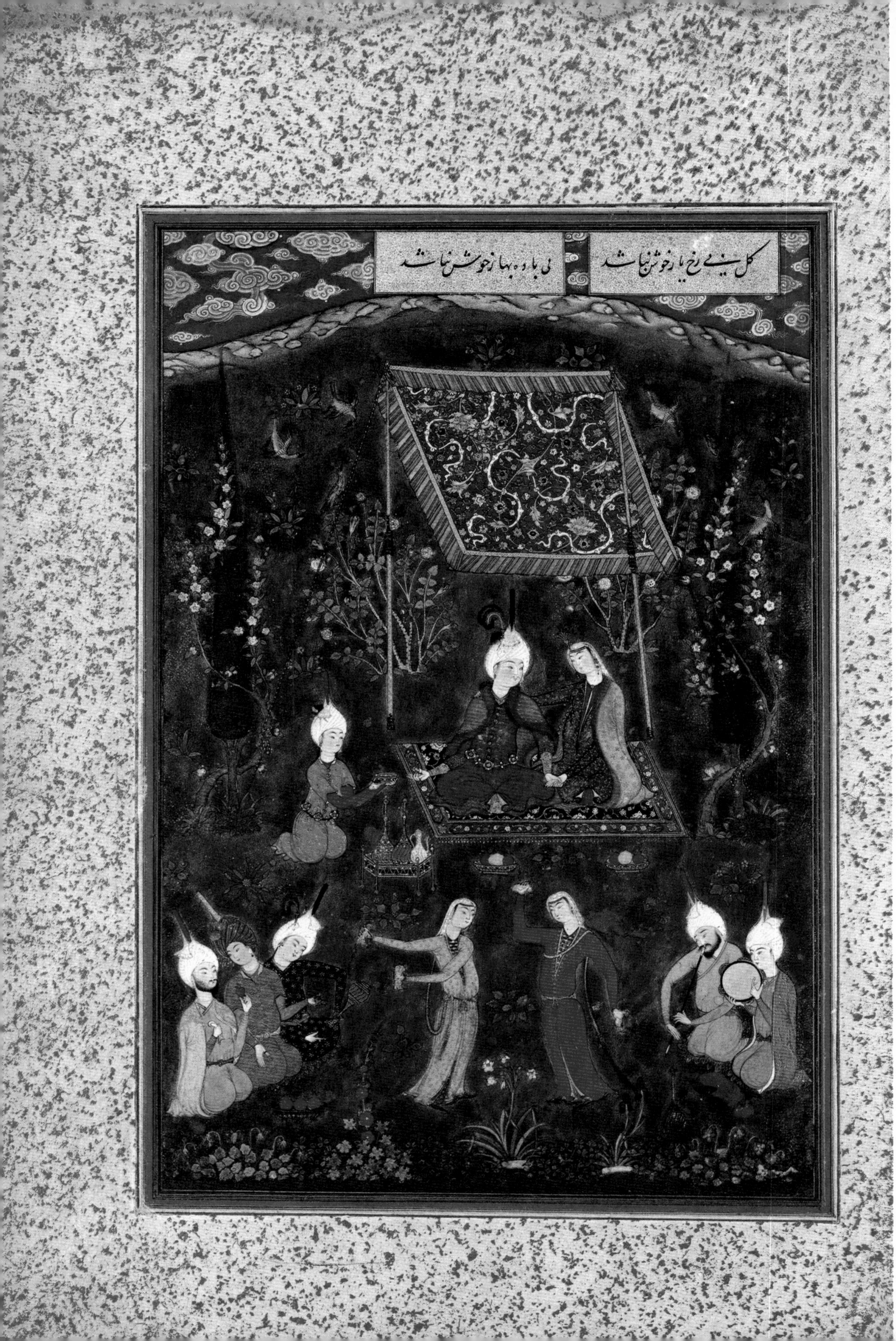
گل بی رخ یار خوش نباشد
بی باده بهار خوش نباشد

Diwan of Hafiz*

PLATE 15, folio 67 recto

Lovers Picnicking

ATTRIBUTABLE TO SULTAN-MUHAMMAD

How can the rose be beautiful without the cheeks of the beloved?
And without wine, of what use is spring?
Basking on the lawn and breathing garden air are joyless unaccompanied
by tulip cheeks.
For there is no beauty apart from her embraces and sugar-lipped kisses.
True, her dances are lacking without the songs of nightingales;
But even masterful painting is drab when she is not the subject.
Without love-making, the garden, roses, and wine are joyless;
But your two-bit life, Hafiz, is an unworthy love offering!

One of the most lyrical and amorous of Iranian pictures, it is nevertheless devoid of sentimentality. Although he employed the trite Iranian metaphor of showing the lovers' faces round as full moons, Sultan-Muhammad expressed their passion symbolically in the lightninglike arabesque of the canopy.

* All miniatures from the Diwan manuscript are reproduced in their actual size.

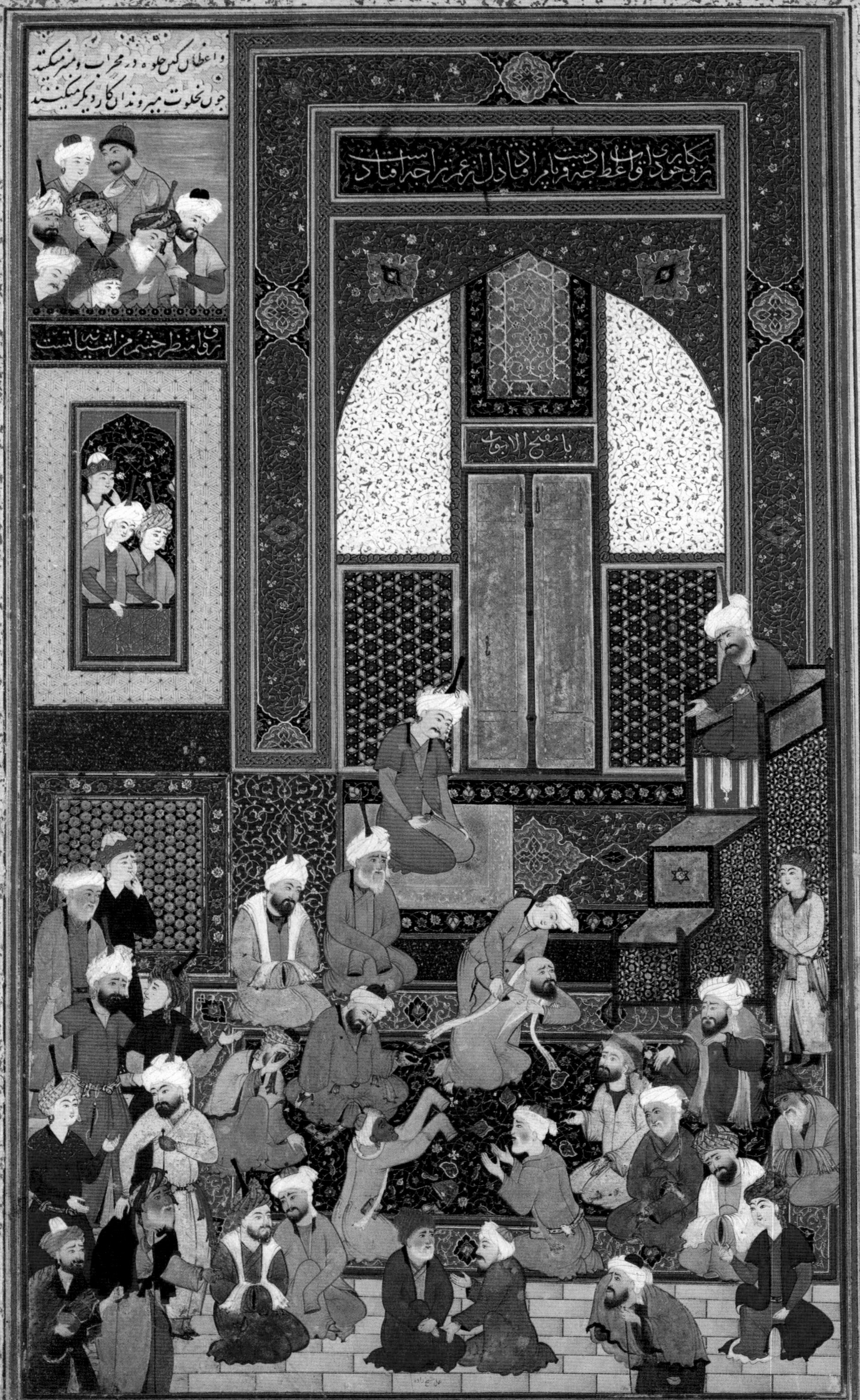

واعظان کین جلوه در محراب و منبر میکنند
چون بخلوت میروند آن کار دیگر میکنند
رواق منظر چشم من آشیانهٔ تست
یا مفتح الابواب

PLATE 16, folio 77 recto

Scandal in a Mosque

SIGNED BY SHAYKH ZADEH

Pious and proud in their prayer arches and pulpits,
In private they make work of quite another kind.
Why do those who order penitence of others
Make penitence so seldom themselves?

Unquestionably Shaykh Zadeh's masterpiece, this brilliantly designed and finished miniature is also the largest in the *Diwan.* Seemingly, the artist strove to outmatch the great Sultan-Muhammad; but his efforts failed. Underappreciated, he soon left the Safavid court and went to Bukhara.

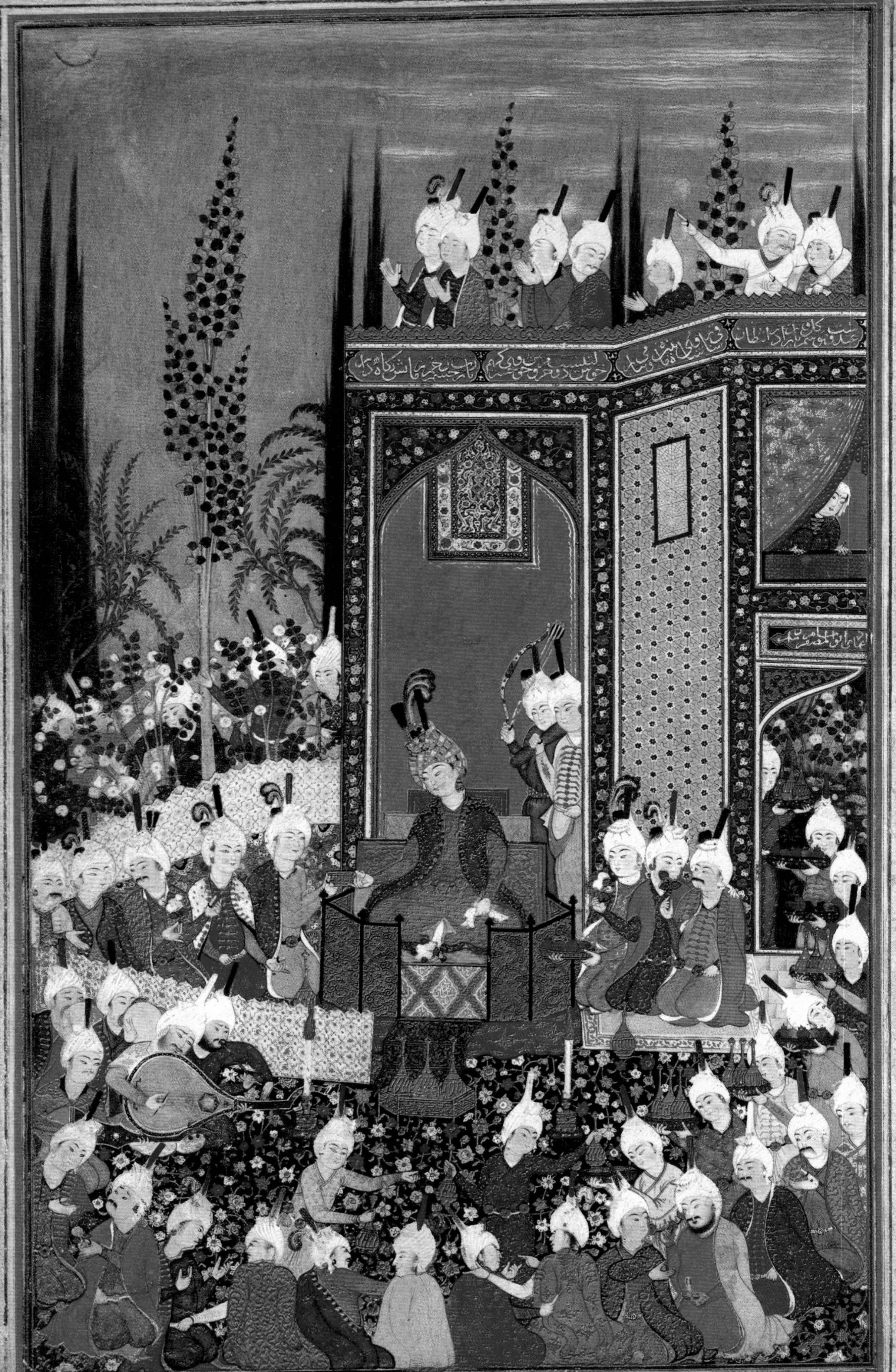

PLATE 17, folio 86 recto

The Feast of 'Id Begins

SIGNED ON THE THRONE BY SULTAN-MUHAMMAD

Roses and friends eagerly await, for it is the time of 'Id.
Saki! (wine bearer) Behold the refulgent moon in the king's resplendent face and bring wine!
(Verses written on right side of architectural frieze.)

He is fortunate, a noble ruler,
Oh God, Spare him from the evil eye.
(Verses written on left side of architectural frieze.)

'Id, the feast marking the end of the fast of Ramadan, begins at the moment when the new moon is sighted. The artist's earthy sense of humor, reminiscent of his hunting scene in the Paris manuscript (Plate 13), spoofs the celebration, particularly in the portrayal of the moon-watchers on the rooftop. One is grimly serious, two others stifle yawns, while a pair of lovers are otherwise preoccupied. Below, the host (presumably Prince Sam Mirza, whose name and title are inscribed above the archway to the right) oversees a gathering of courtiers, some of whom are entwined with roses in a botanical arabesque, while slightly porcine waiters begin to distribute wine and sweetmeats.

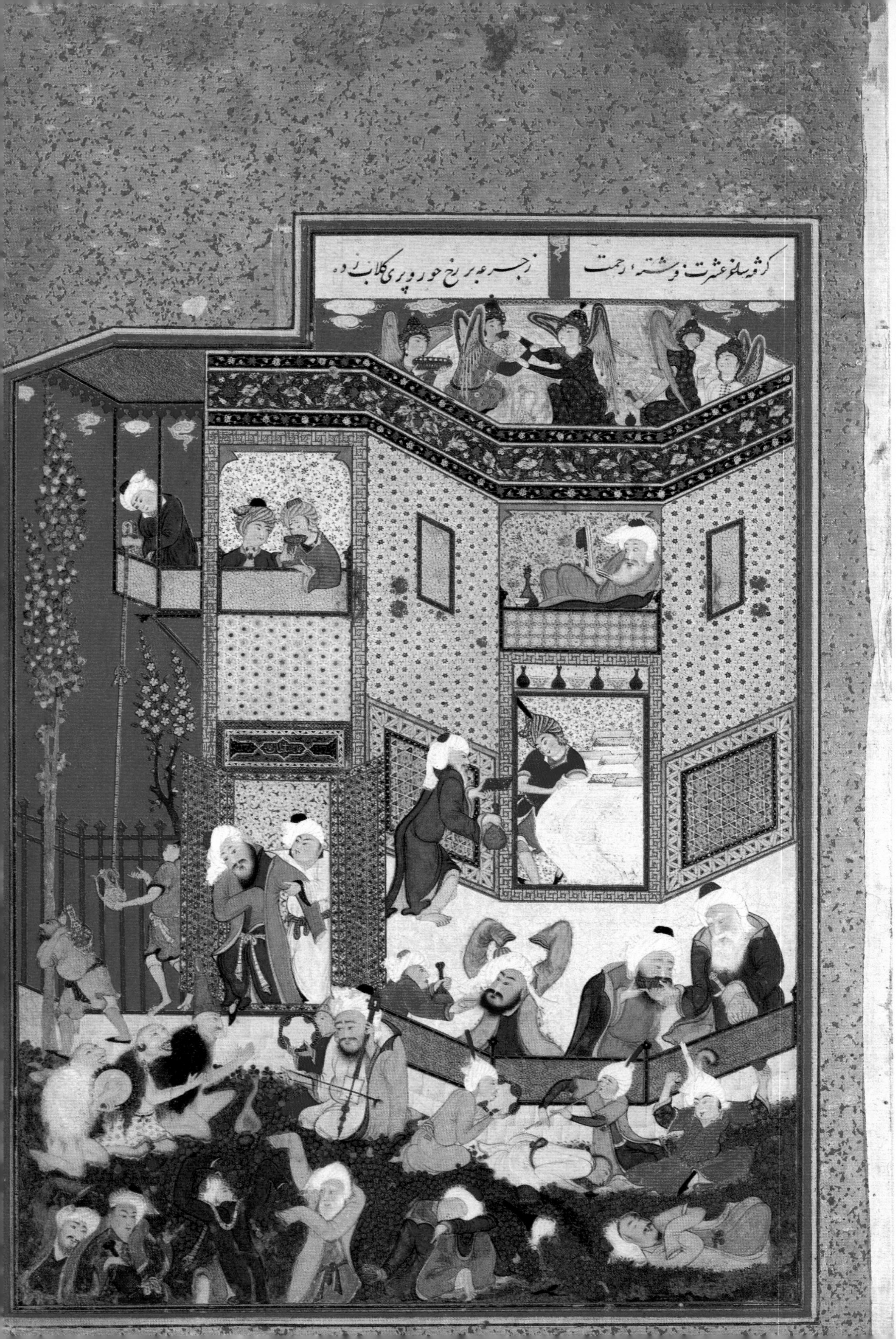
گرفته ساغر عشرت فرشته رحمت
ز جرعه بر رخ حور و پری گلاب زده

PLATE 18, folio 135 recto

Worldly and Otherworldly Drunkenness

SIGNED ABOVE THE DOORWAY, LEFT:
"THE WORK OF SULTAN-MUHAMMAD 'IRAQI' "
(SIGNIFYING HIS ADHERENCE TO THE WESTERN TRADITION
OF IRANIAN PAINTING)

Hafiz's lines, inscribed above the painting, set the theme:

"The angel of mercy took the cup of reveling."

Sultan-Muhammad's and Hafiz's Sufism join in a perfect union of spirituality and comedy, the worldly and the heavenly. Hafiz himself, popeyed with booze or religious inspiration, sits in a window above the huge wine jars. Nearby, a reluctant boy furrows his brow over his first taste of wine, or ecstasy, while below, more experienced celebrants dance, tipple, stagger, and fall into happy obliviousness. To the left, three outlandish musicians, dressed in woolen garments, shriek and clang. Presumably they are *qalandars* (extremist mystics) whose presence lends wildness to the poet's gathering.

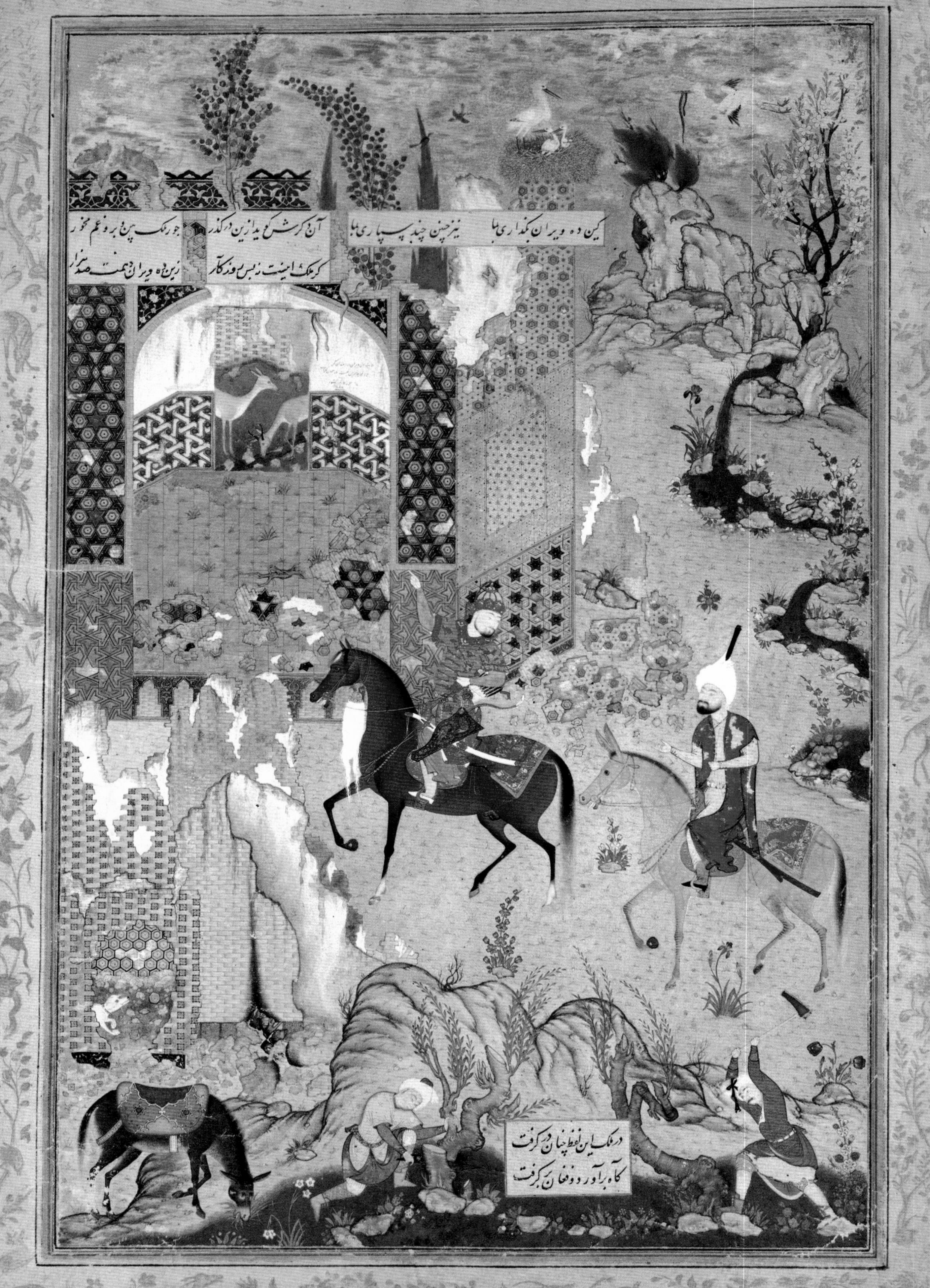
کین ده ویران بگذاری بما
نیز چنین چند سپاری بما
آن دگرش گفت کزین درگذر
جور ملک بین و برو غم مخور
گر ملک اینست نه بس روزگار
زین ده ویران دهمت صد هزار
در ملک این لفظ چنان درگرفت
کآه برآورد و فغان برگرفت

Khamsa of Nizami

PLATE 19, folio 15 verso

Nushirvan Listening to the Owls on the Ruined Palace

ATTRIBUTABLE TO AQA MIRAK

Nushirvan was a great king, who sometimes forgot that his glory as a warrior and huntsman was at the expense of his people. One day, while riding with his vizier, he came upon a ruined town where two owls were hooting at one another from a crumbling palace wall. "What secrets are they telling one another?" asked Nushirvan. "Pardon me, O King, for repeating their remarks," replied the vizier. "One of them is giving his daughter in marriage to the other and is demanding a suitable dowry. 'Give her,' he says 'this ruined village and one or two others thrown in.' 'By all means,' replies the other. 'If our noble ruler continues in his present course, leaving his people to perish in misery and neglect, I will gladly give not two or three but a hundred thousand ruined homes!' "

PLATE 20, folio 15 verso

Nushirvan Listening to the Owls on the Ruined Palace/detail, *Deer and ruin*

ATTRIBUTABLE TO AQA MIRAK

The nostalgia of ruins has seldom been expressed more movingly than here, in one of the most romantic of Iranian pictures. Nevertheless, the *Khamsa* to which it belongs represents the most classical moment in Safavid painting, a crystalline, logical, technically refined phase in which cerebral and emotional elements combine in perfect balance.

The palace wall is inscribed "Erected in the deserted heart of those deprived of happiness, there is no better edifice than this. Written by Mi. . . . Musavvir, 946 A.H. (1538/39 A.D.)." The signature, partly damaged by flaking, is apparently that of Mir Musavvir (see Plate 1), whose son Mir Sayyid 'Ali (see Plate 28) probably worked long and hard finishing this magnificent miniature which was designed and largely executed by Aqa Mirak, an older master who got all the credit for it. Mir Musavvir's verses would seem to refer to his son's unacclaimed but superb accomplishment. For other pictures by Aqa Mirak see Plates 22, 23, 30, 31, Figures d, e, f, w and x.

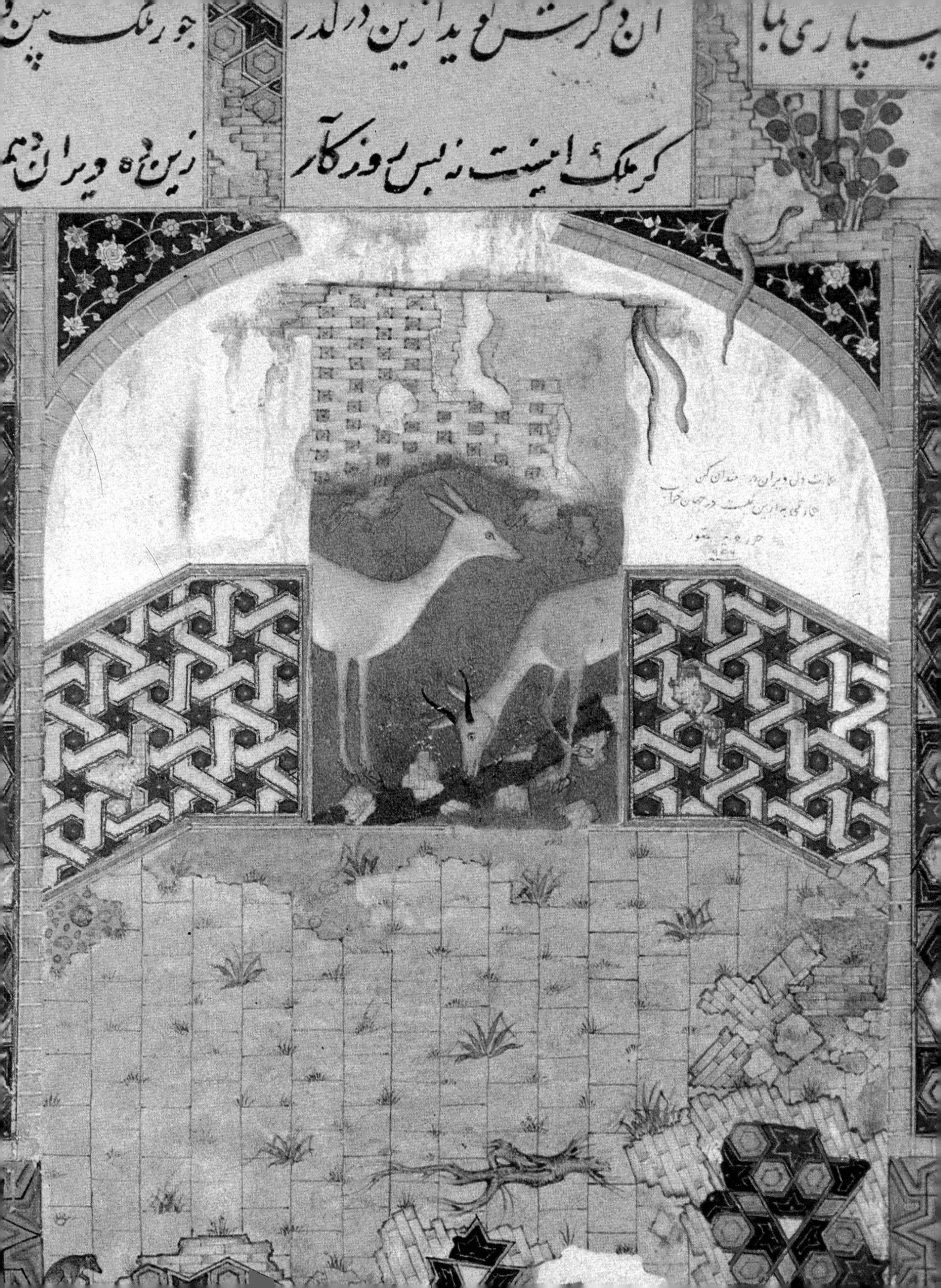
کر ملک اینست نه بس روزکار

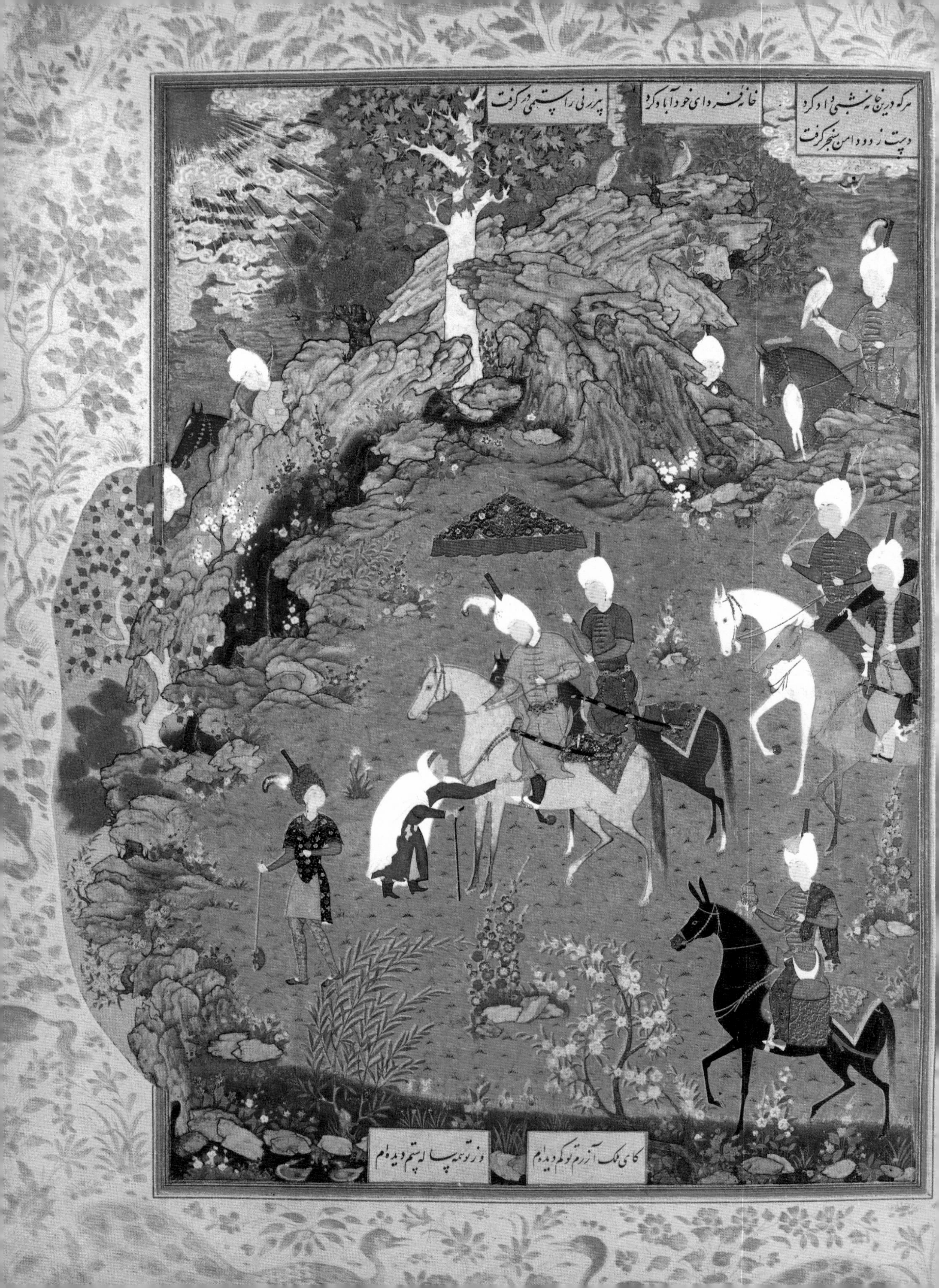
هر که درین خانه شبی داد کرد
خانهٔ فردای خود آباد کرد
دست زد و دامن سنجر گرفت
پیرزنی را ستمی درگرفت
کای ملک آزرم تو کم دیده‌ام
وز تو همه ساله ستم دیده‌ام

PLATE 21, folio 18 recto

The Old Woman Complaining to Sultan Sanjar

ATTRIBUTABLE TO SULTAN-MUHAMMAD

Sultan Sanjar, a ruler of the Seljuks from 1119 to 1156, was stopped one day by an old woman who complained that she had been robbed by one of his soldiers. Annoyed by her words, he answered, "How can you bother me with your trivial complaints? Can't you see that I am setting forth on a campaign to conquer and punish the whole world?" "What is the use," she countered, "of conquering foreign armies when you are unable to make your own behave?"

Although painted in the refined style of the later 1530s and 40s, the rocks in this miniature are as ghoulishly populated as those in *The Court of Gayumarth* (Plates 2, 3). Some, indeed, contain as many as three distinct animal and human profiles.

Like others in this well-worn, much admired book, the border of this picture was replaced in the late seventeenth century, at which time the left edge was somewhat insensitively trimmed.

PLATE 22, folio 26 verso

The Physicians' Duel

ATTRIBUTABLE TO AQA MIRAK

Rival physicians demonstrated their powers at court. The first prepared a terrible pill, compounded of ingredients intended to rend stomachs and kill with convulsions. His opponent swallowed it with a smile, along with a bolus of his own creation that rendered it as harmless as a lump of sugar. Then it was his turn. He walked over to a flower bed, plucked a rose, breathed a spell onto it, and handed it to the first. The other had watched his progress nervously; but he popped it into his mouth and fell down dead.

Aqa Mirak, typically, illustrated the story with elegance, drama, and extraordinary refinement. Although the triumphant physician's crocodile grimace and hand clap first draw our attention, our eyes are lured into exploring each flower, vessel of fruit, or immaculately wound turban. The picture is also rewarding as an accurate description of the costumes, noblemen, and setting at Shah Tahmasp's court.

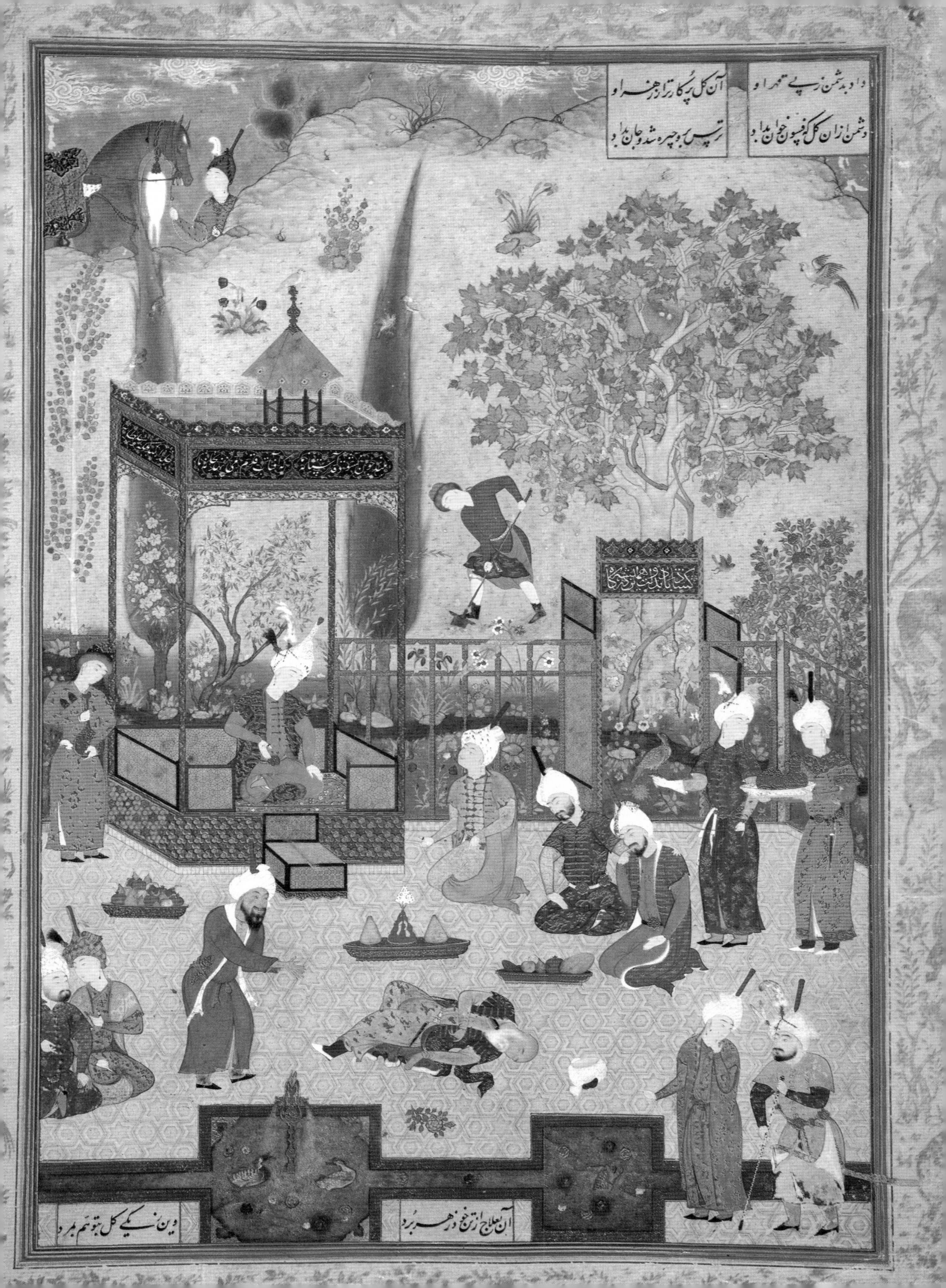
داد بدشمن ز پی قهر او
دشمن از آن گل که فسون خوان بداد
آن گل پرکارتر از زهر او
ترس بر او چیره شد و جان بداد
آن بعلاج از تن خود زهر برد
وین ز یکی گل بتوهم بمرد

PLATE 23, folio 26 verso

The Physicians' Duel/detail, *Intertwined trees and figures beneath them*

ATTRIBUTABLE TO AQA MIRAK

Although such details as this are delightful to linger over, they tend to lead us to other centers of interest because they are dynamic parts of carefully balanced harmonies. Aqa Mirak's designs, with their artfully placed "spots," such as the trees, throne area, physicians, and clusters of noblemen, remind us of a juggler tossing lemons, limes, and pineapples into the air. Neither the artist nor the performer ever seems to fail, but they always keep us in suspense.

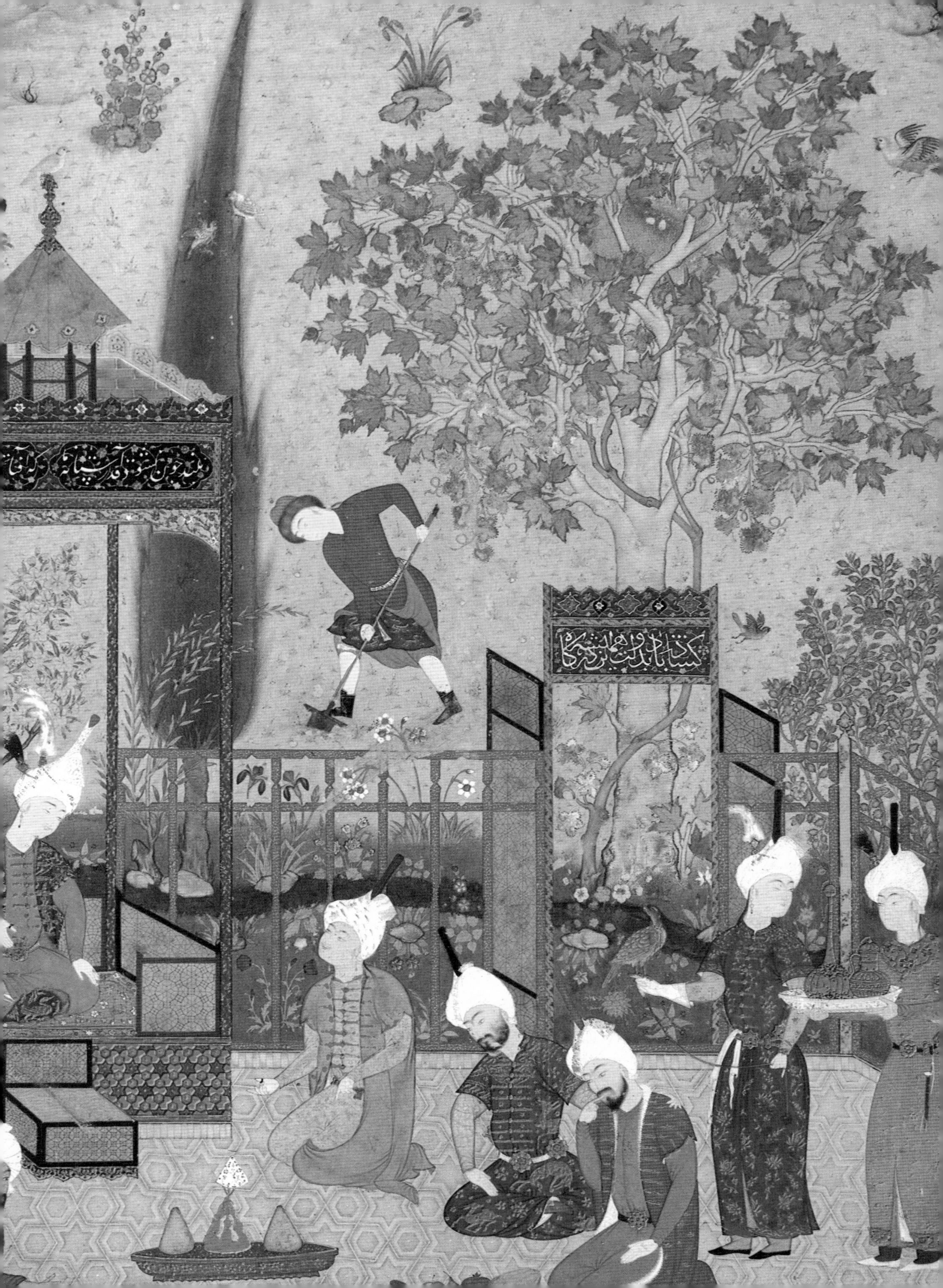

PLATE 24, folio 48 verso

Nushaba Recognizing Iskandar from His Portrait

ATTRIBUTED TO MIRZA 'ALI

Something went wrong. Although the lines of text belong to the story of Shirin and Khusraw, the picture does not. To fit the words, it should depict Shirin falling in love with Khusraw from a portrait of him hung on a tree in a garden by his friend Shapur (see Plate 25; for another episode in this long tale, see Plate 12). This miniature, however, is a court scene and must represent Nushaba recognizing Alexander the Great from his portrait. When the *Khamsa* was refurbished in the late seventeenth century, several miniatures were removed from the volume, fresh borders were made as substitutes for worn ones, and—it appears—this picture was moved to its present position from the section of the book that tells the tale of Alexander.

Mirza 'Ali described the quirks and foibles of the Safavid courtiers more fully and observantly than any other of Shah Tahmasp's artists. His portraitlike characterizations probably show actual members of the Shah's circle. Although psychologically revealing, they are never unkind.

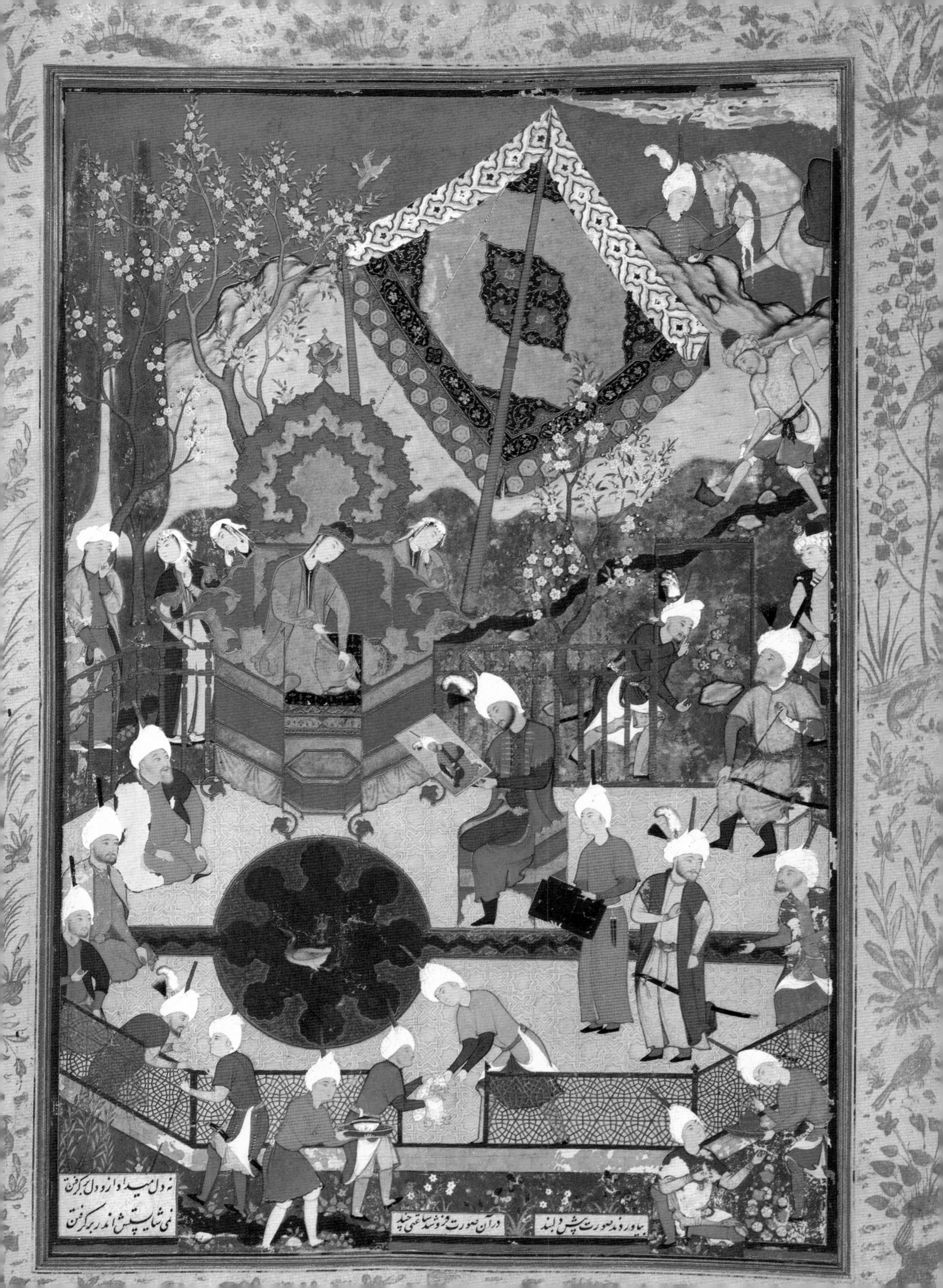

بیاوردند صورت پیش دلبند
در آن صورت فرو شد ساعتی چند
نه دل میداد ازو دل بر گرفتن
نمی‌شایستش اندر بر گرفتن

PLATE 25, folio 53 verso

Shirin Bathing

ATTRIBUTED TO SULTAN-MUHAMMAD

The lengthy, frustrating love affair between Prince Khusraw of Iran and Shirin, an Armenian princess, began with his falling in love with a description of her beauty by his friend Shapur, who was then sent to Armenia where he showed her the portraits of Khusraw that inspired the princess's love. By then, they were so eager to meet one another that she rushed to Iran and he bolted for Armenia.

Shirin rode her night-black horse, Shabdiz, for seven days and nights, until at last, dusty from travel, she bathed in an inviting pool. While she was doing so, Khusraw, en route to Armenia, chanced upon the disarming scene, upon which he gazed as though in a trance. For a moment, in extreme embarrassment, each sighted the other. And although each sensed the other's identity, they were both too overcome to speak. They rode on.

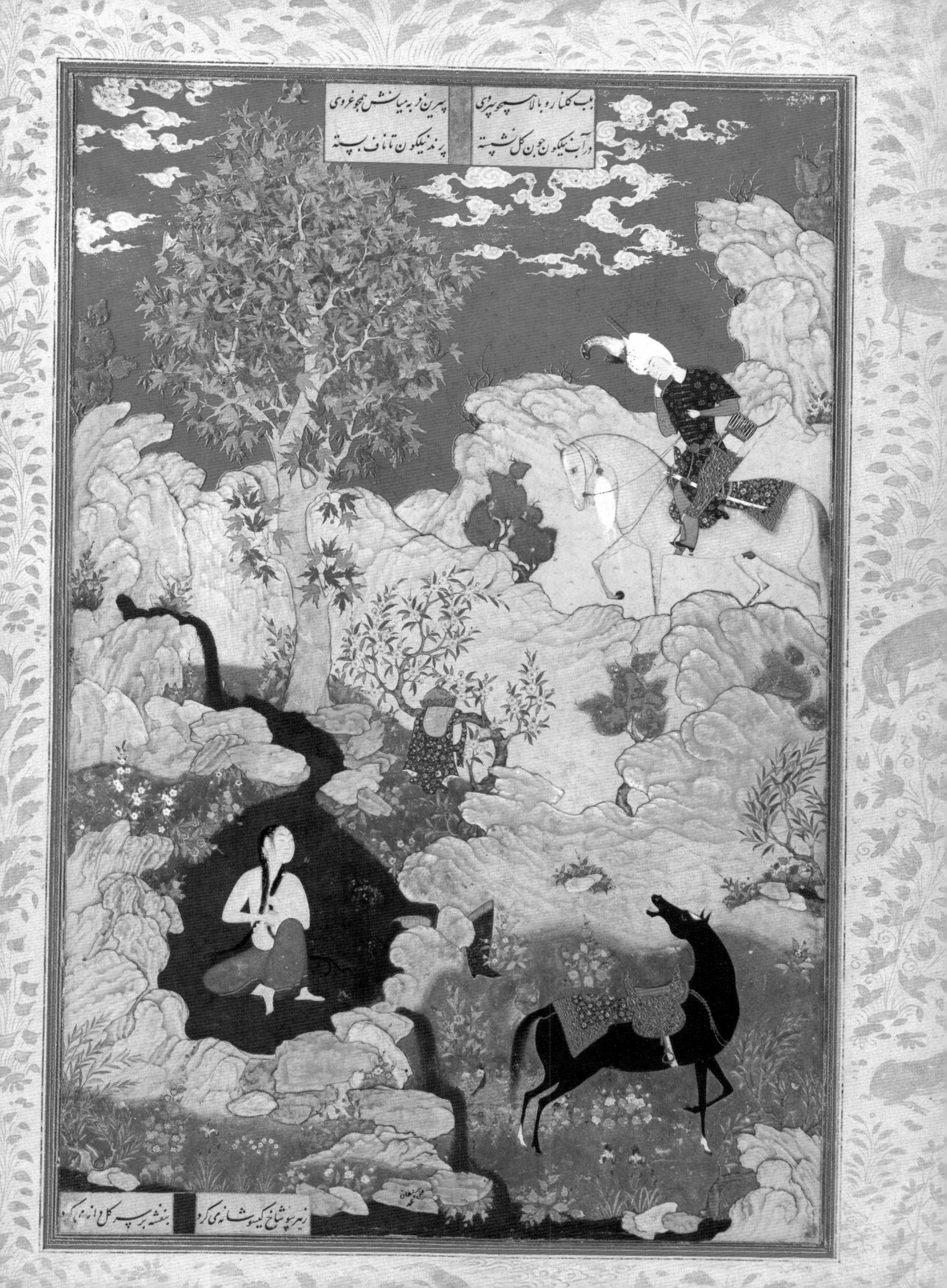

درآب نیلگون چون گل نشسته
پرندی نیلگون تا ناف بسته
زهر سو شاخ گیسو شانه می کرد
بنفشه بر سر گل دانه می کرد

PLATE 26, folio 77 verso

Barbad Playing Music to Khusraw

ATTRIBUTED TO MIRZA 'ALI

After many near encounters and misunderstandings, Khusraw and Shirin finally met and spent many blissful months together. Particularly agreeable diversions were serenades by proxy in which either Shirin's singer voiced the princess's love for Khusraw, or Barbad, his favorite musician (see Plate 10) sang ballads to Shirin. Here, the Iranian prince and his friends, including Shapur at the extreme right, listen to Barbad, who is perhaps rehearsing a love song for Shirin. The nurse and the boy shooting an arrow may allude, in fact, to a future tragedy. For Khusraw's wife Miriam bore him a son who grew up, fell in love with Shirin, and had his father murdered. The story ends with Shirin entering Khusraw's tomb and stabbing herself to death. At last they were united.

This and several other miniatures in the *Khamsa* bear reliable if not contemporary attributions to their artists, written either in the margins or on the pictures themselves.

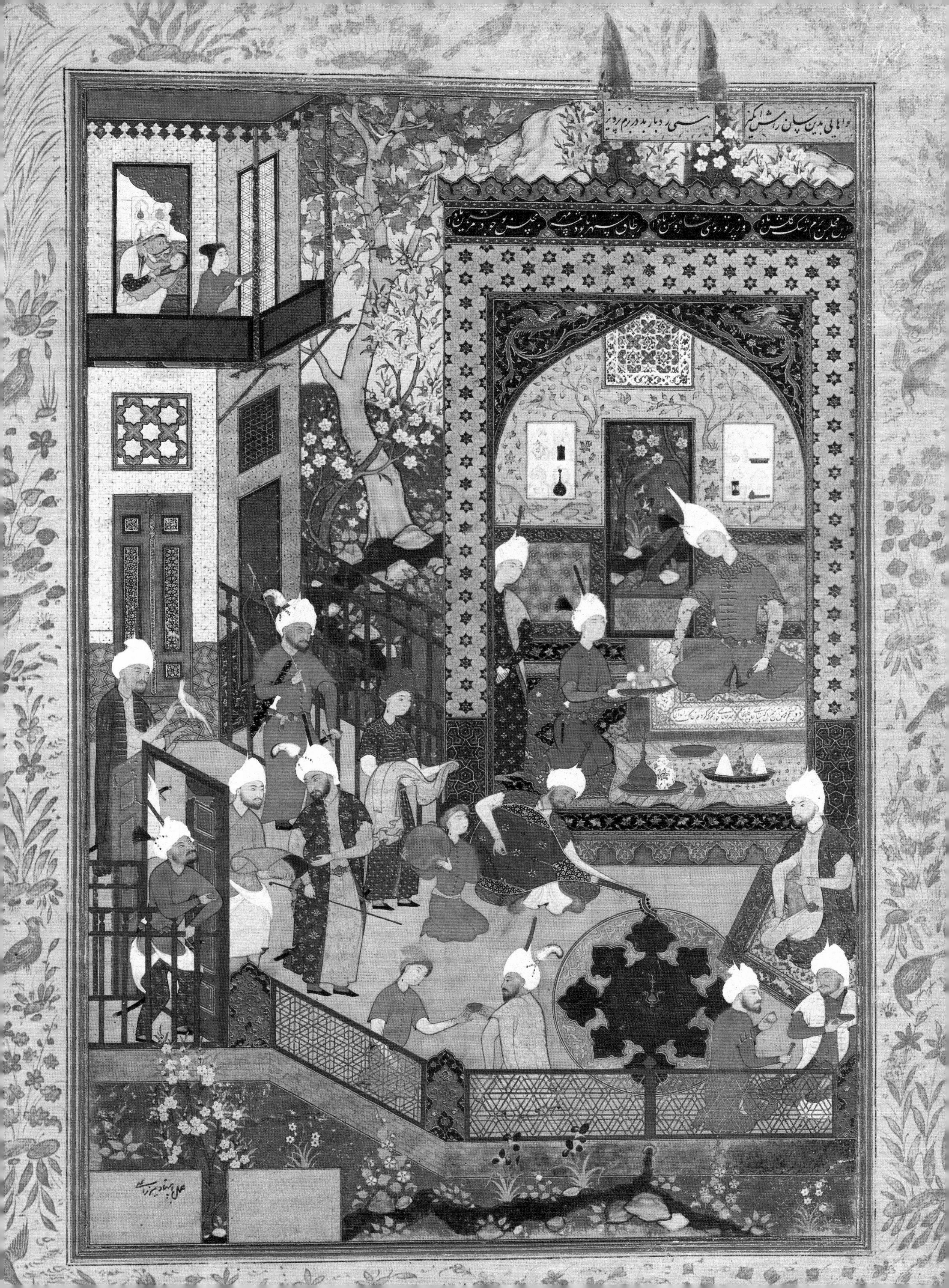

PLATE 27, folio 77 verso

Barbad Playing Music to Khusraw/detail, *Musicians and two figures seated below them*

ATTRIBUTED TO MIRZA 'ALI

Although it has been claimed that Shah Tahmasp's artists worked so uniformly that their individual idioms are unidentifiable, close observation of their pictures brings out many clues by which one can separate the different hands. Mirza 'Ali, for instance, can be singled out not only from his attitudes towards man and nature, his compositional devices, his repetition of certain personality types, and his ornament, but also by such small details as his particularly neatly tied turbans, most of which bulge with the same tortoiselike curves.

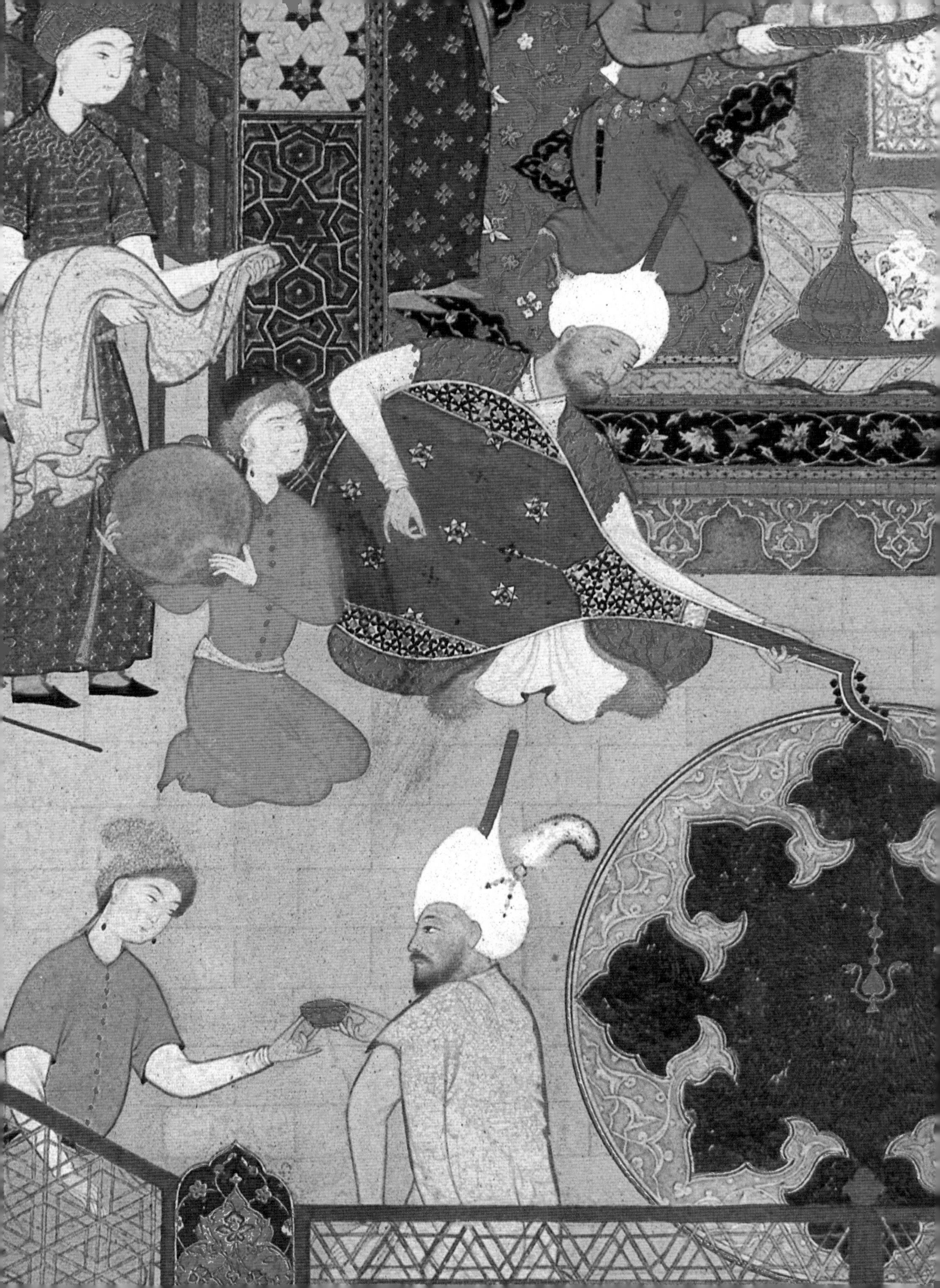

PLATE 28, folio 157 verso

Majnun in Chains Brought by a Beggar Woman to Layla's Tent

ATTRIBUTED TO MIR SAYYID 'ALI

The story of Layla and Majnun invites comparison to Romeo and Juliet, for the Iranian lovers also met while very young, came from families traditionally hostile to one another, and died tragically at an early age. Although his given name was Qays, it was changed to Majnun ("the Madman") after he had fallen crazily in love with Layla, whom he encountered at school. Because her family detested his, they could seldom meet, and he was forced to extreme lengths in order to gain glimpses of her. Here, he is shown disguised as a mad beggar boy chained to his keeper. Unfortunately, although this ruse was well-planned, his feigned madness turned into true madness when he neared Layla's tent. He became so excited that he broke his chains and the plot was discovered.

Mir Sayyid 'Ali, son of Mir Musavvir, was one of the most inventive designers and meticulous craftsmen of the Safavid school. His textile patterns and still-life objects are precisely observed and scrupulously painted. Often, they show us things that have not otherwise survived.

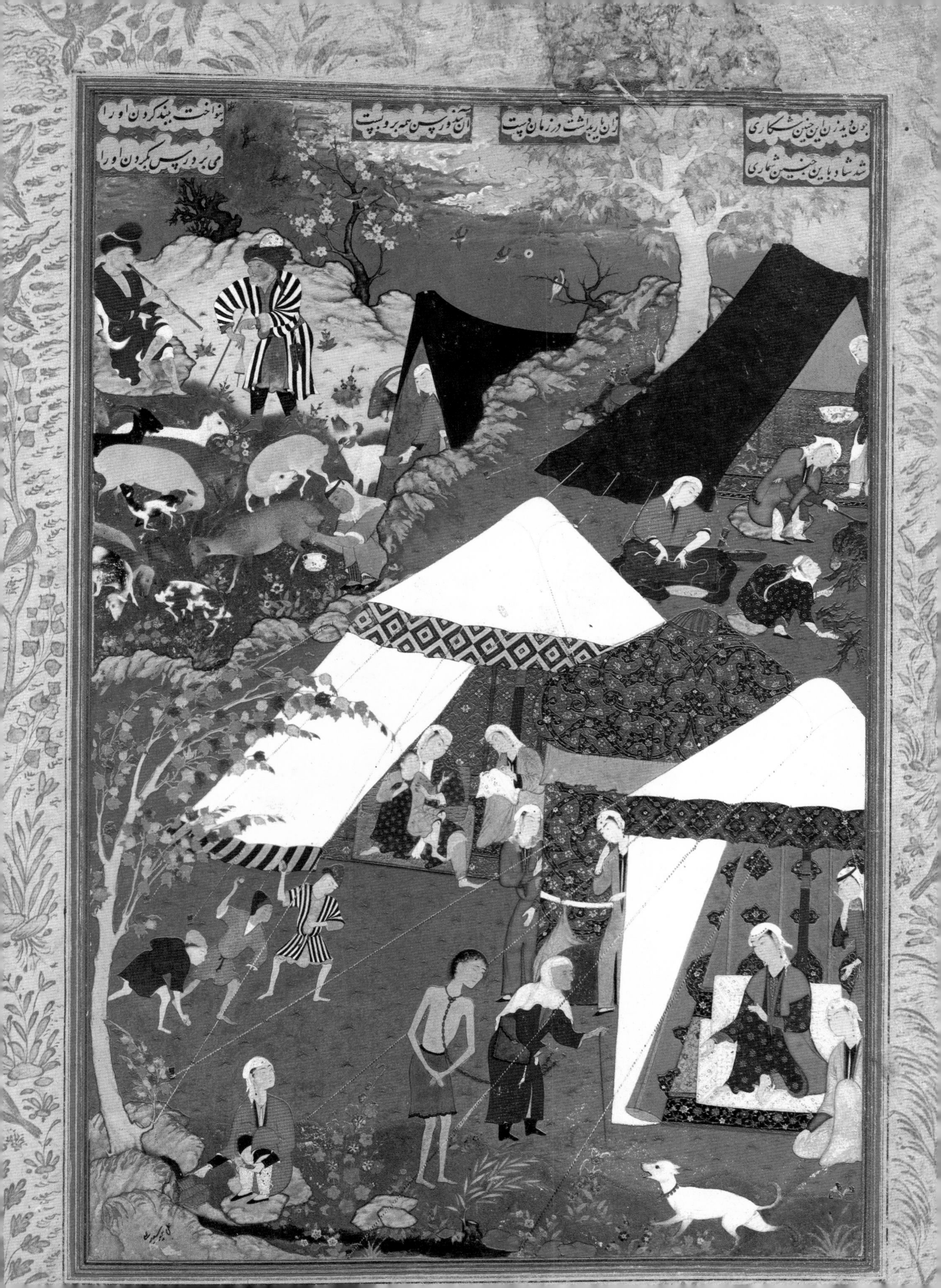

چون دید زن این چنین شکاری
شد شاد باین چنین شماری
بنواخت بند گردن او را
می برد درپس بگردن او را

PLATE 29, folio 157 verso

Majnun in Chains Brought by a Beggar Woman to Layla's Tent / detail, *Four women and tents*

ATTRIBUTED TO MIR SAYYID 'ALI

In Mir Sayyid 'Ali's pictures, even the smallest, humblest items are beautiful, due to his uncanny sense of abstract pattern. We especially admire the scraps of broken firewood which are harmonized by underlying arabesque rhythms. Note, too, the compacted yet gracefully shaped girl blowing on the flames, a virtual human bellows.

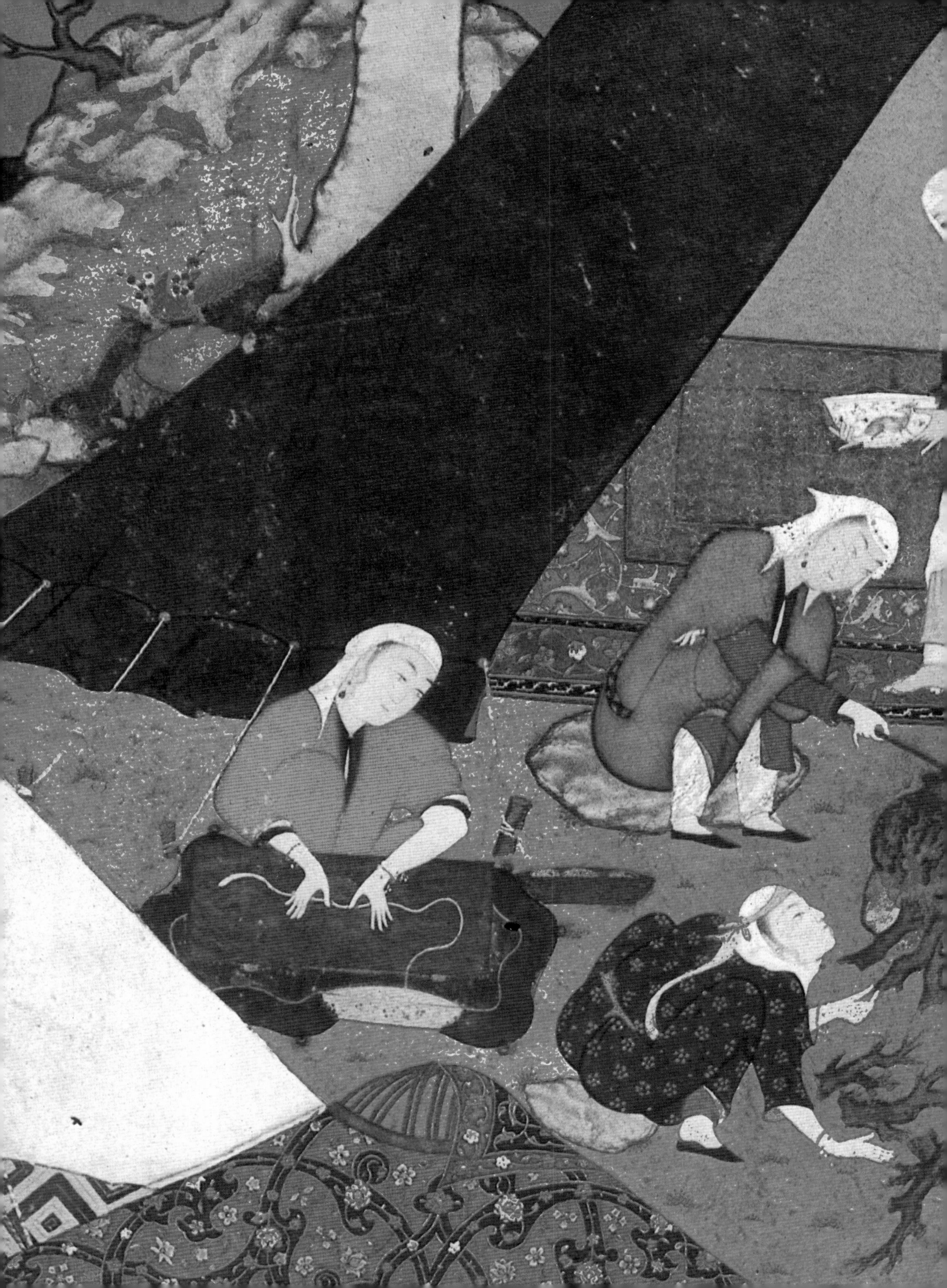

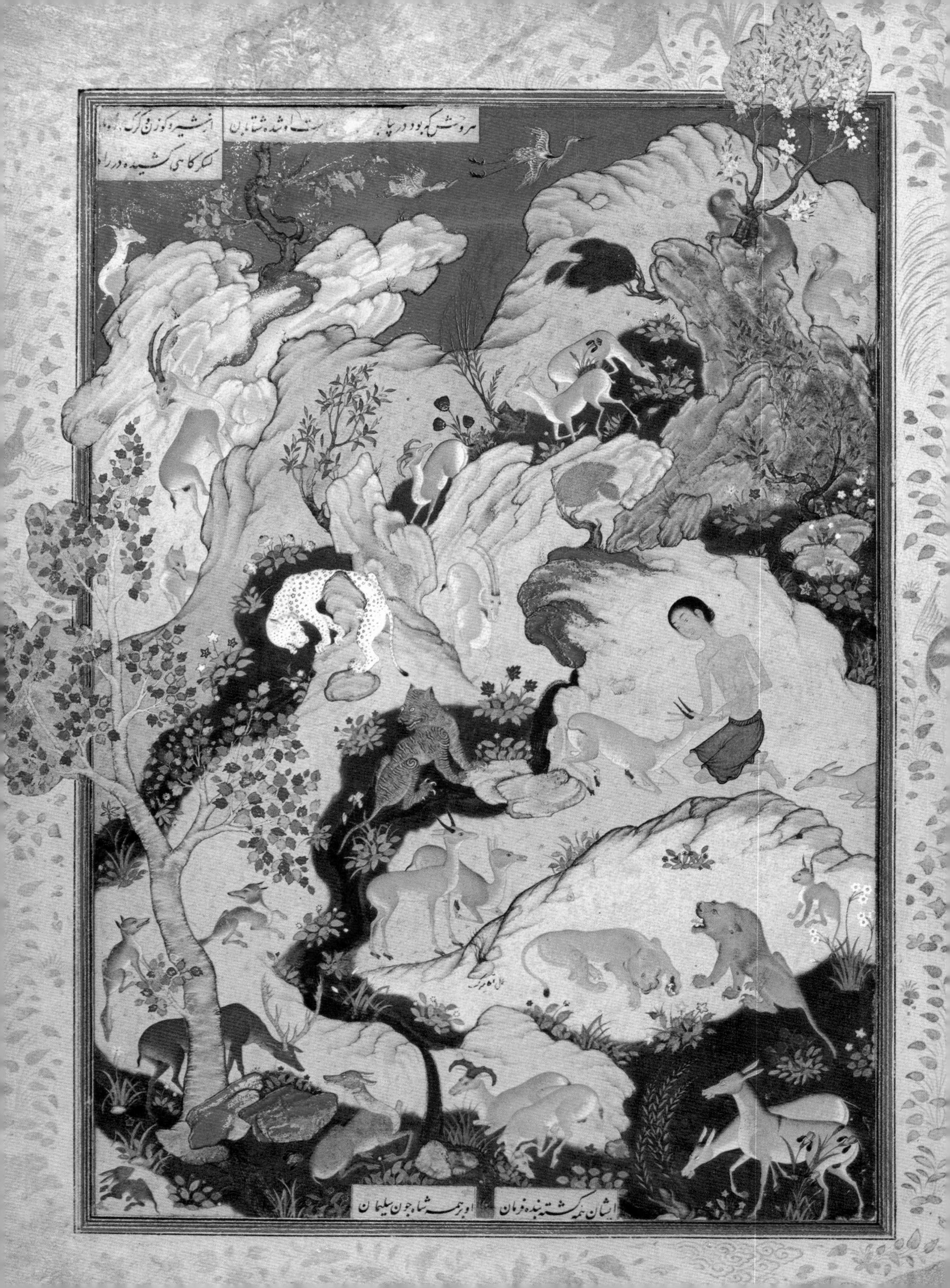

از شیر و گوزن و گرگ
لشکرگاهی کشیده در راه
شده شتابان
ایشان همه گشته بنده فرمان
او بر همه شاه چون سلیمان

PLATE 30, folio 166 recto

Majnun in the Desert

ATTRIBUTED TO AQA MIRAK

Like Sir Lancelot, the love-mad Majnun fled to the wilds where his sole companions were animals. But unlike the Arthurian knight, whose filthy beard and scraggly hair were alarmingly uncouth, the Iranian lover seems to have been further refined by the experience. Here, he is as gently graceful as the antelope he strokes.

For this flowing, idyllic landscape with its sinuous stream, bright flowers, and pleasing arrangement of birds and beasts, Aqa Mirak has devised a shimmering palette of cool, pale blues, violets, greens, tans, and gold. The perfection of these hues recalls that Shah Tahmasp put him in charge of procuring all the precious materials used to make such pigments in the royal ateliers.

Overleaf

PLATE 31, folio 166 recto

Majnun in the Desert/detail, *Snow leopard, tiger, and mountain goat*

ATTRIBUTED TO AQA MIRAK

Aqa Mirak's refinement and humor, qualities which must have contributed to his success at the Safavid court, are notably apparent in this detail. The mountain goat, looking as edible as a delicious bun, tiptoes precariously down the steep rocks, while the snow leopard and tiger hiss at one another with unexpected decorum. The latter, in tribute perhaps to the art of China so beloved by the Safavids, sports the symbolic Taoist whorl of yang and yin on his shoulder and leg.

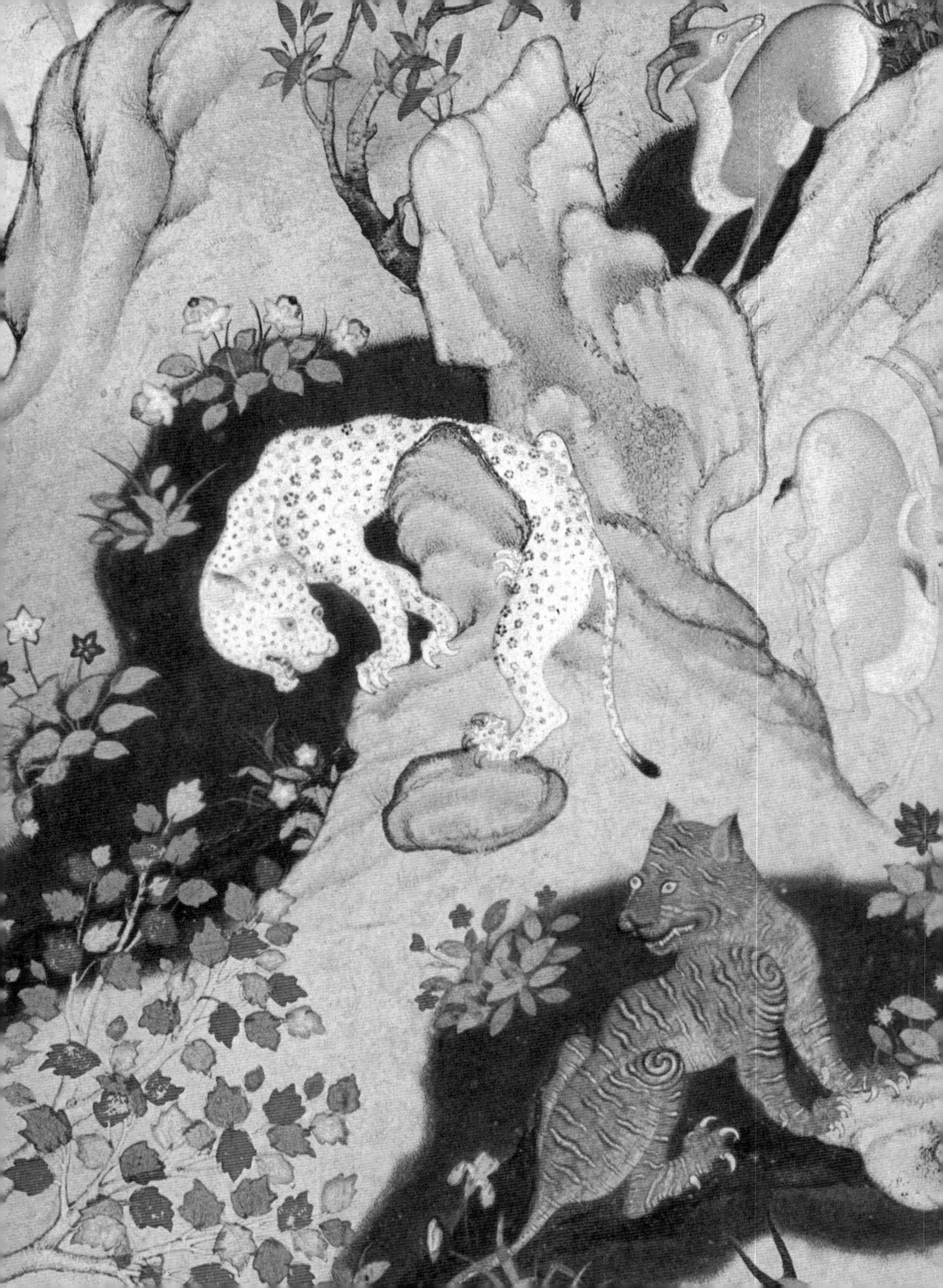

Overleaf

PLATE 32, folio 195 recto

The Ascent of the Prophet to Heaven

ATTRIBUTABLE TO SULTAN-MUHAMMAD

On a starry night, while still alive, the Prophet Muhammad freed himself of this world and rode upwards accompanied by angels into heaven on his human-headed steed Buraq. There he beheld the majesty and presence of God.

If this awesome painting is valid evidence, Sultan-Muhammad had experienced such a vision. Its spiritual, ascending forms, dragonlike wisps of cloud, flapping angel wings, and electrifying bursts of flame catch us up in the Prophet's flight. Nevertheless, it maintains contact with Shah Tahmasp's court—for the Prophet himself wears the Safavid turban, and the angels and Buraq are dressed for court.

PLATE 33, folio 195 recto

The Ascent of the Prophet to Heaven/detail, *The angel in front of the Prophet, and the head and forequarters of Buraq*

ATTRIBUTABLE TO SULTAN-MUHAMMAD

Although the Prophet himself was too sacred to be painted, and is shown veiled, Buraq's face combines angelic innocence and the utmost aristocratic elegance. Through the sputter of heavenly flame the beckoning angel's wings are visible, recalling the most marvelous of sunrises in their coloring and the most awesome of mountain peaks in their shapes.

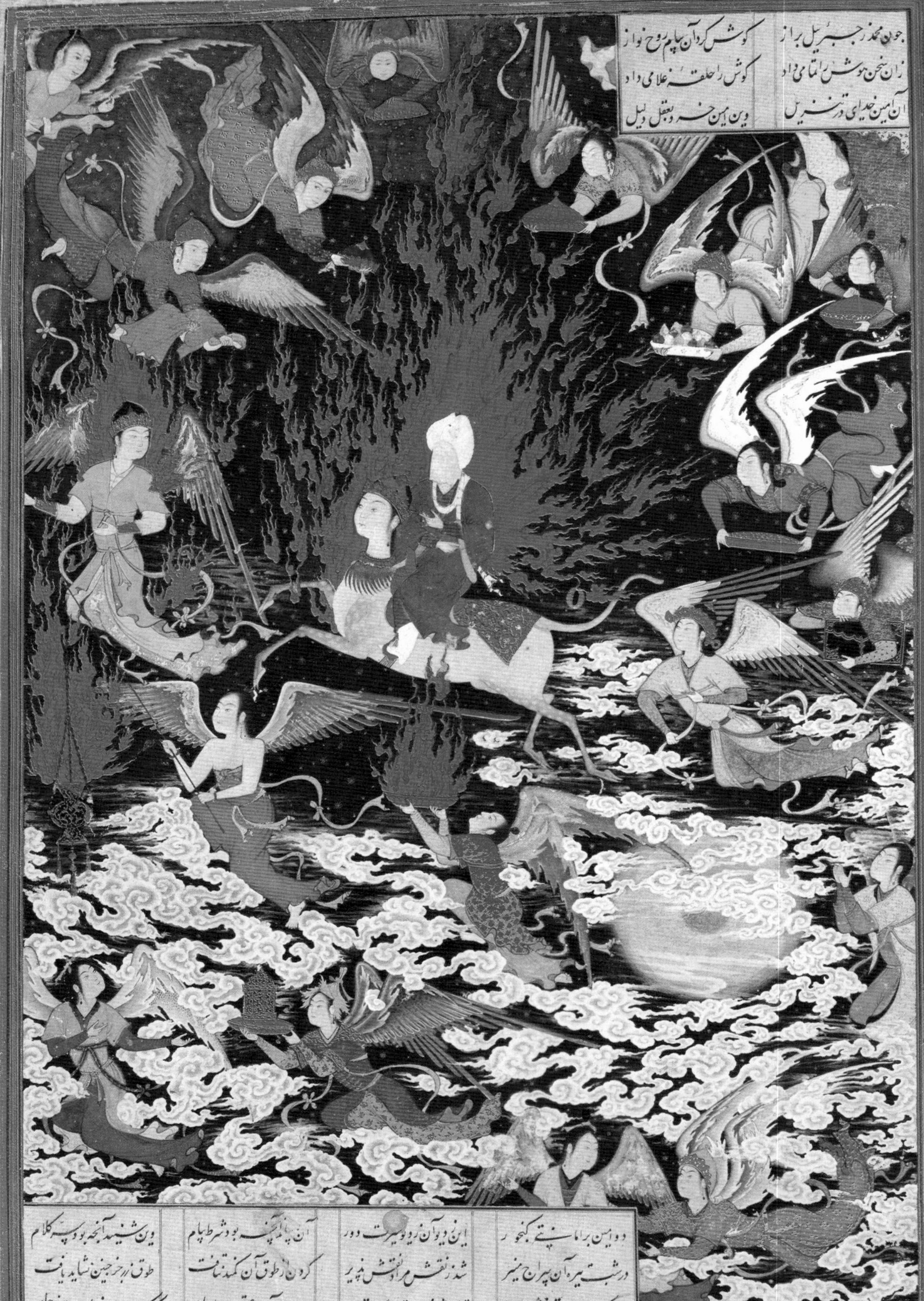
چون محمد ز جبرئیل براز
گوش کرد آن پیام روح نواز
زان سخن هوش را تمامی داد
گوش را حلقهٔ غلامی داد
آن امین خدای در تنزیل
وین امین خرد بعقل دلیل
دو امین بر امانتی گنجور
این ز دیو آن ز دیو سیرت دور
در شب تیره آن چراغ منیر
شد ز نقش مراد نقش پذیر
برق کردار بر براق نشست
آن پیامی که بود شرط پیام
وین شنید آنچه بود پیر کلام
گردن از طوق آن کمند نتافت
چون درآورد بر عقیلی پای
کبک علوی خرام جست ز جای

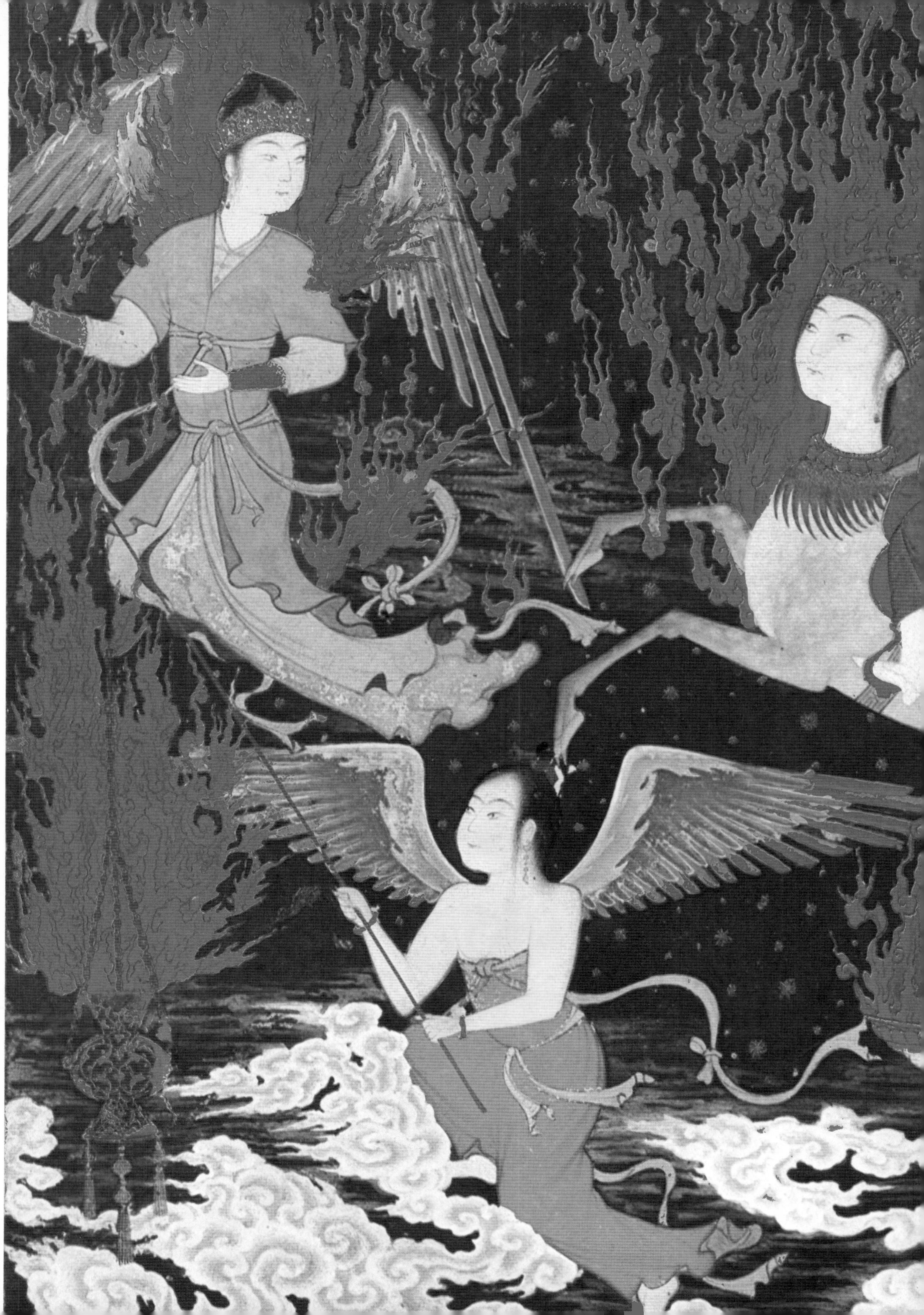

Haft Awrang of Jami

PLATE 34, folio 38 verso

"Donkey for Sale!"

ATTRIBUTABLE TO MIRZA 'ALI

Many of the illustrations for the *Haft Awrang* stray from simplistic story telling even more than those for the British Museum *Khamsa* (Plates 19–33). In this picture the actual subject is an anecdote about a peasant who brings to market a broken down old donkey and outrages prospective purchasers by describing its strength and beauty, qualities no longer evident. Nearby, contrasting with the sadly emaciated animal, Mirza 'Ali has painted a proudly galloping young nobleman, almost certainly a portrait of Ibrahim Mirza, who would have been about sixteen years old when this miniature was made for his splendid manuscript.

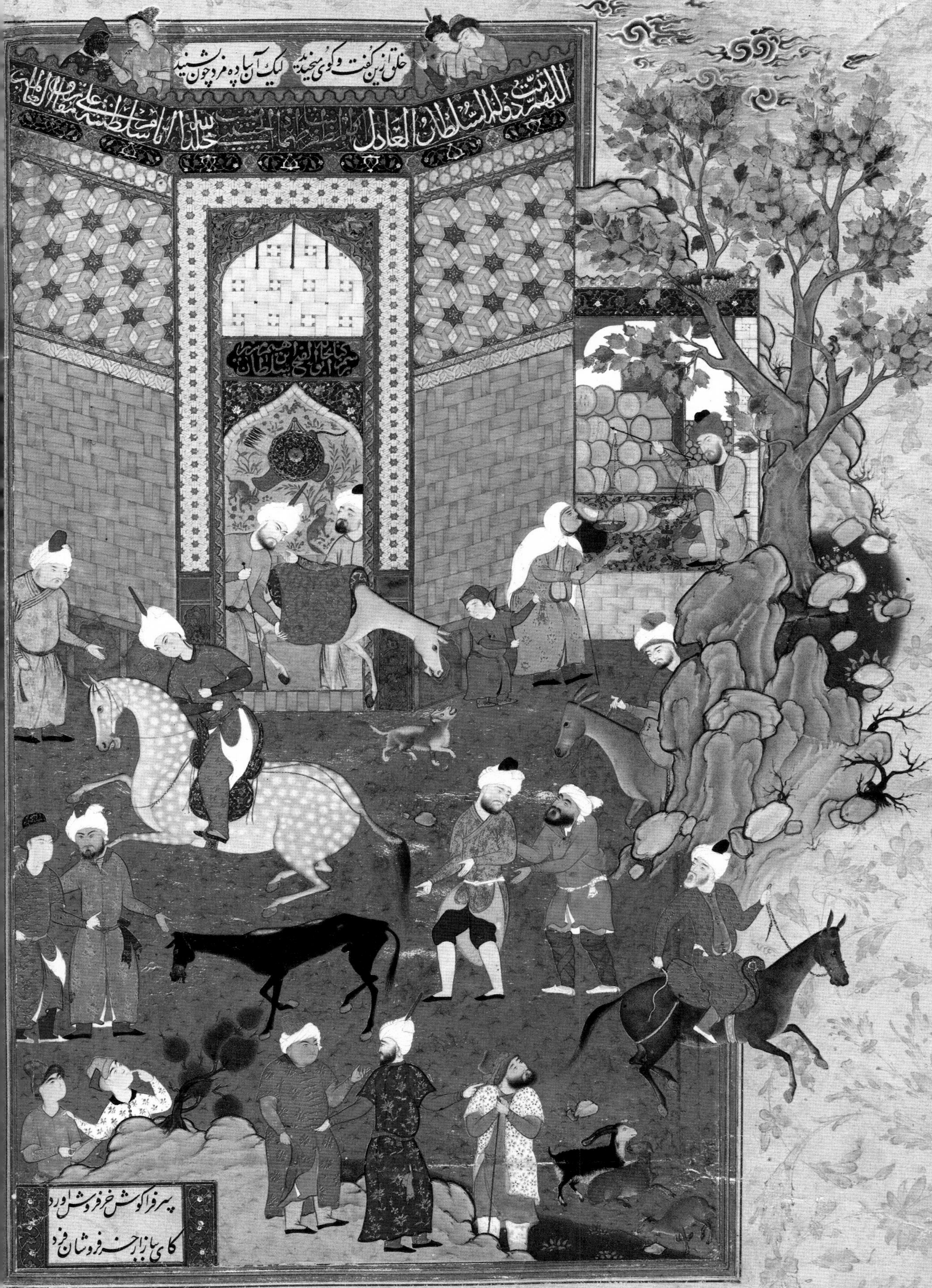

PLATE 35, folio 38 verso

"Donkey for Sale!"/detail, *Sultan Ibrahim Mirza (?) and emaciated donkey*

ATTRIBUTABLE TO MIRZA 'ALI

Mirza 'Ali's powers of observation enabled him to paint one of the liveliest and most accurate equestrian portraits in Safavid art. The young sultan and his springingly vital charger bound through the busy marketplace. Despite the unhappy note of the pained old donkey, this picture is joyous and evokes the young patron's excitement in 1556 when he had been appointed governor of Mashhad and been given the use of his uncle the Shah's greatest artists and calligraphers. This miniature was one of the first fruits of a new and intensely productive phase of Safavid patronage.

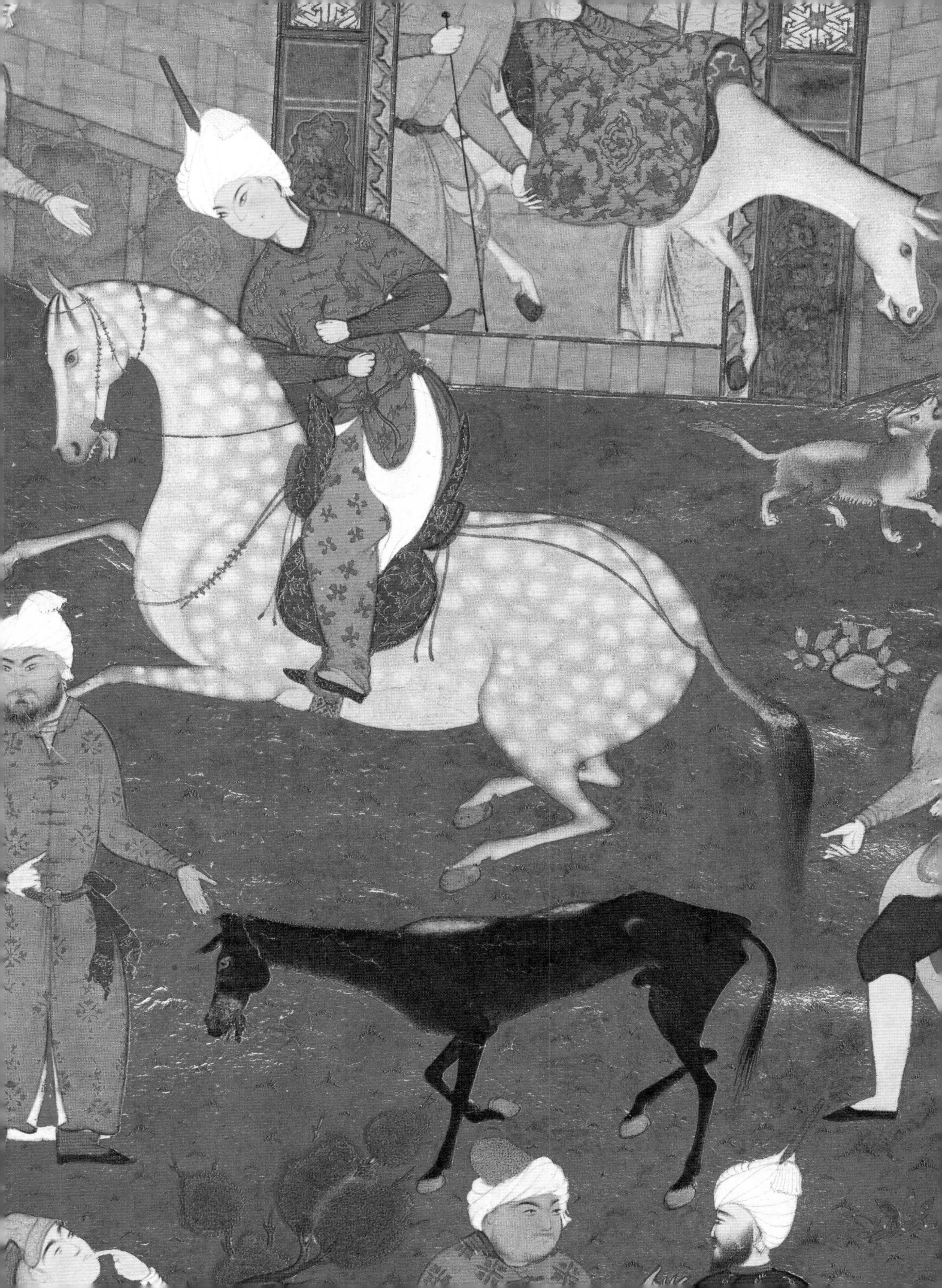

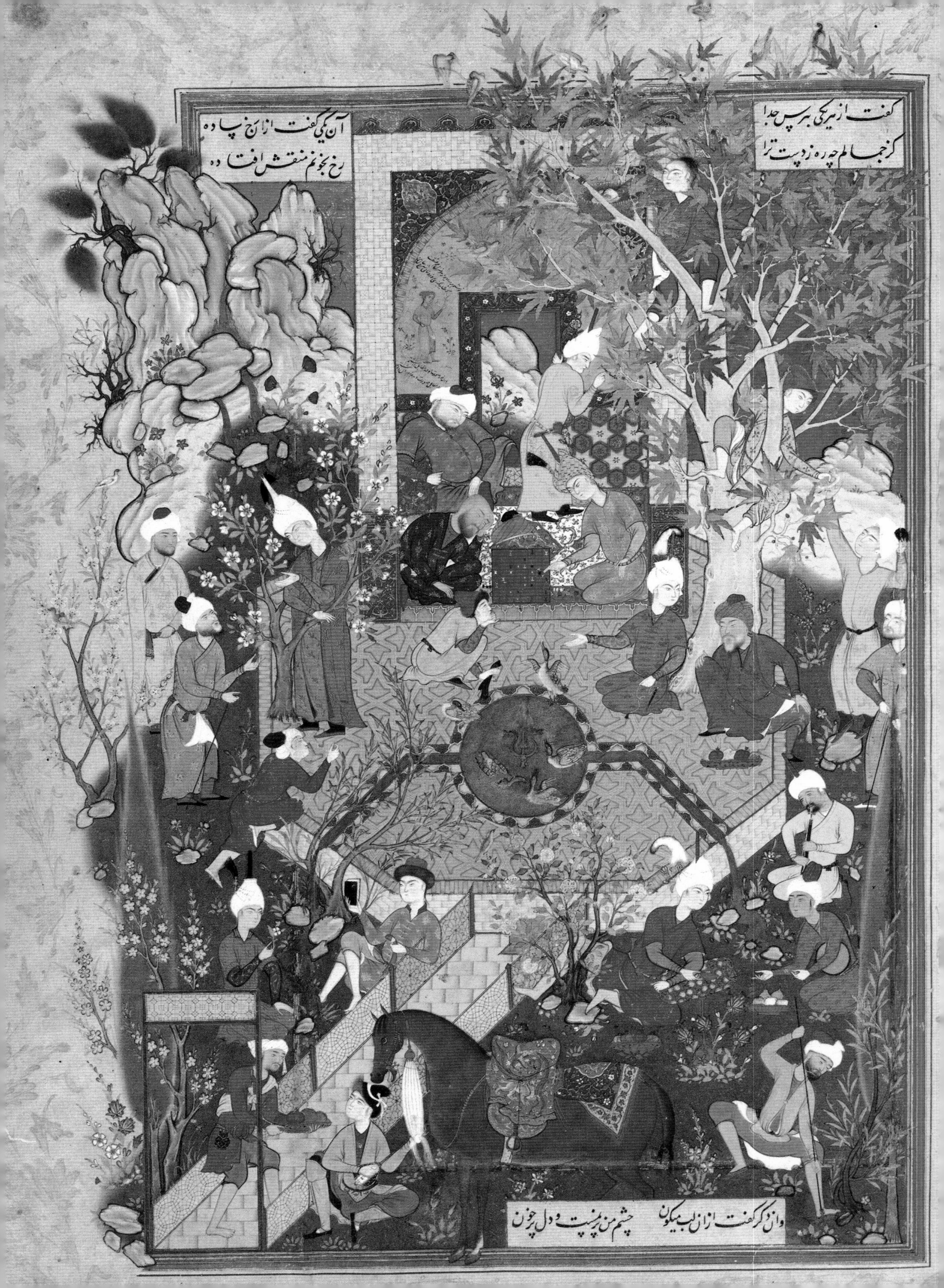
آن یکی گفت از رخ پیاده
رخ بنجوم منقش افتاده
گفت از زیرکی بر پس جدا
گر جمالم چه ره زد پت ترا
وان دگر گفت ازان لب میگون
چشم من پر ز پشت و دل پر خون

PLATE 36, folio 52 recto

A Father's Discourse on Love

ATTRIBUTABLE TO MIRZA 'ALI

Again the artist takes us into the private world of his princely patron—in this case into a splendid garden, with flowers, a plane tree, and a tiled polygonal platform, complete with pond, fountain, and playful ducks. A large cast of courtiers and attendants enjoys the setting. Some play chess, others listen to music or read; and the more agile climb the tree. Amid all this it would be easy to overlook the theme of the picture, which is a conversation between a father and his eager son, who asks for—and is given—a discourse on love.

If we compare Mirza 'Ali's paintings for the *Khamsa* (Plates 24 and 26) with these for the *Haft Awrang,* it is clear that he has become freer and less formal, partly, no doubt, in response to the youthful fun of Sultan Ibrahim's court in contrast to that of the increasingly stern Shah. No art style, however, is ever static, and the Safavid idiom had now passed the classical phase of the *Khamsa* and was moving quickly away from the logical, consistent, harmonious, restrained, and subtle ways of the 1540s.

PLATE 37, folio 52 recto

A Father's Discourse on Love /detail, *Chess players and surrounding area*

ATTRIBUTABLE TO MIRZA 'ALI

With the lessening of restraint came increasing distortions of form, as in the exaggeratedly fat belly of the man watching the chess game. Another change was the introduction of bolder, even excessive, design elements, as here in the dazzling patterns of polygons, rectangles, and curves. In essence, all these innovations marked a turning away from matter-of-fact naturalism.

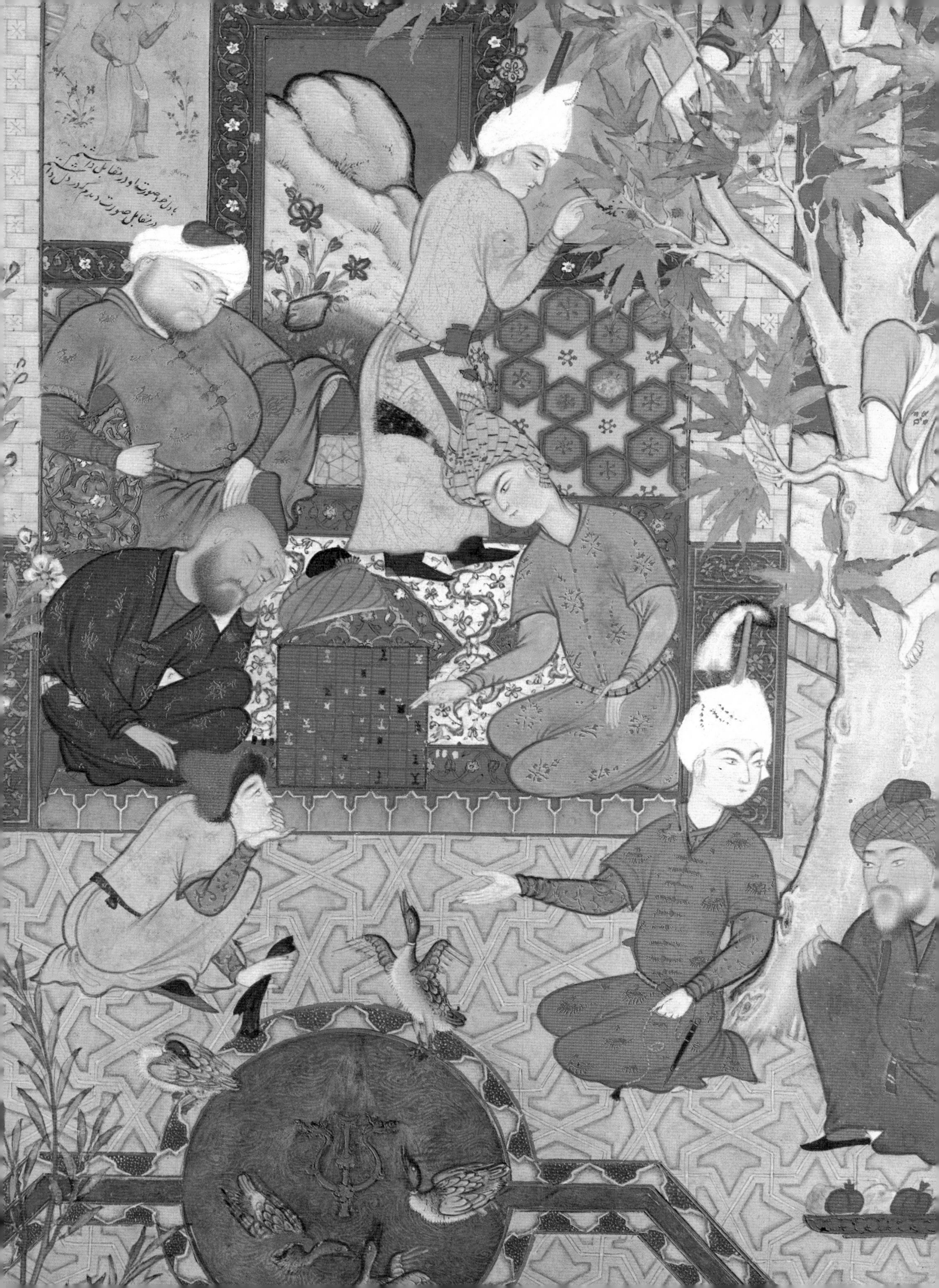

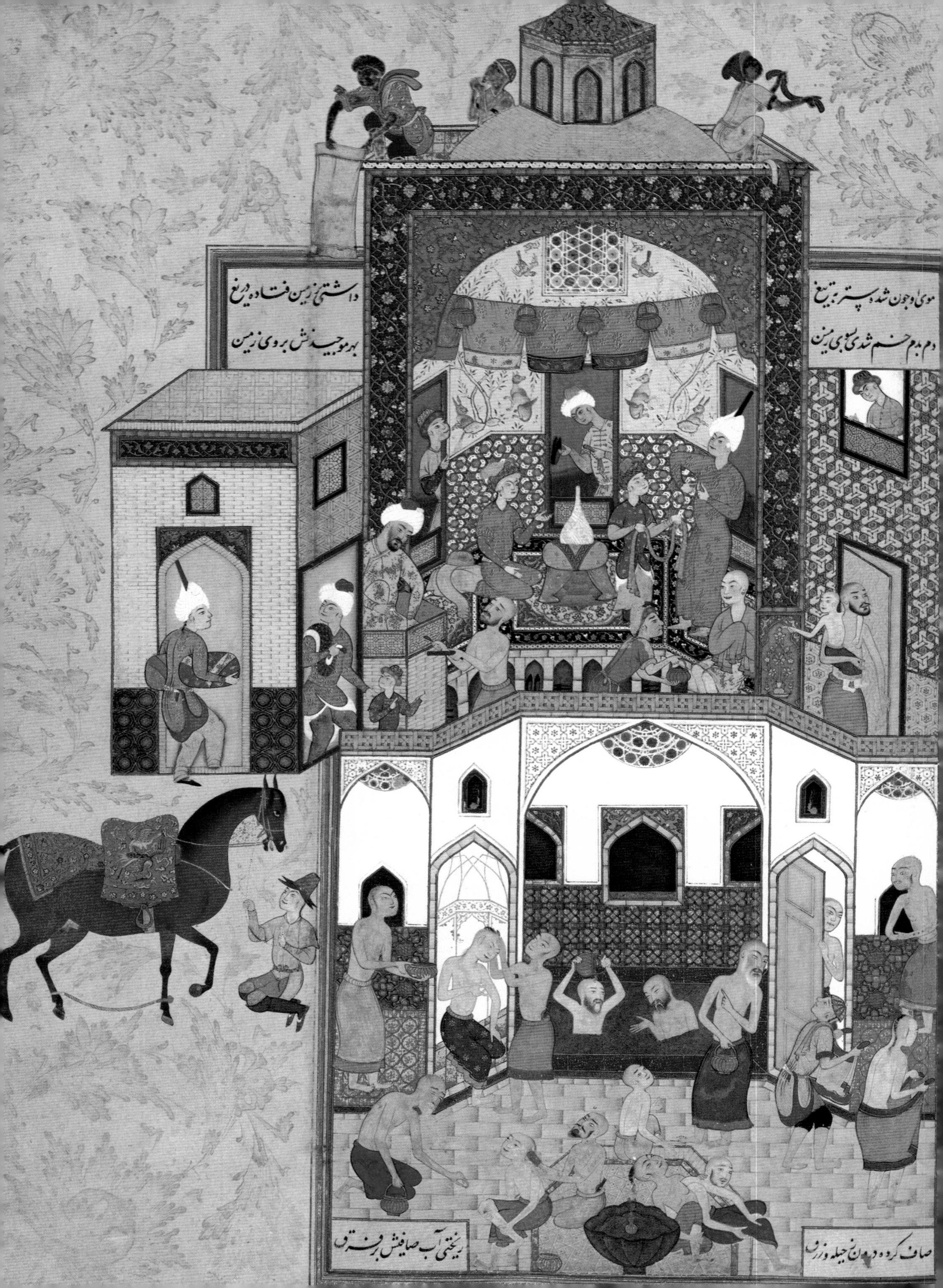
موی او چون شده پستر تیغ
دم بدم خشم شدی بسوی زمین
داشتی بر زمین فتاده دریغ
بهر موچیدنش بروی زمین
صاف کرده درونش حیله و زرق
ریختی آب صافیش بر فرق

PLATE 38, folio 59 recto

Why Is That Sufi in the Hamam?

ATTRIBUTABLE TO PAINTER A, PERHAPS QADIMI

Abu'l 'Ali Rudbasi, a Sufi, was headed for the latrine of the hamam (public bath) when he sighted, hanging in the changing room, the ragged frock of another man of God. Wondering why a Sufi would visit such a place, he investigated and found that the Sufi had fallen in love with a certain youth and gone there to pay him court. Unhappily for the lover, the youth ignored him.

Still intrigued, Abu'l 'Ali folowed the pair when they left the hamam; and he overheard the Sufi asking the young man why he treated him so badly. "I will notice you if you will do me one favor," the youth replied. "What?" said the Sufi. "Die!" (He did.)

Later, Abu'l 'Ali met the same young man, who was dressed as a Sufi. Again he was intrigued, and he asked for an explanation. "After the Sufi's death," the youth told him, "I went to his house and had a vision in which the dead man berated me for worldliness. I repented and became a Sufi."

Painter A was a follower of Sultan-Muhammad whose work can be identified as early as the first phase of the Houghton *Shah-nama*. Always a hearty, comical painter, with a Rabelaisian sense of humor, his ribald spirit shines through here in one of his last pictures, in which he has otherwise adjusted his style to the prevailing manner. Significantly, his slightly coarse technique and view of life must not have appealed to Shah Tahmasp during the years of the *Khamsa*, for none of his miniatures is found in it.

PLATE 39, folio 64 verso

The Murder of Uayna and Raiya

ATTRIBUTABLE TO SHAYKH MUHAMMAD

A sad story, described in true blood-and-guts style by Shaykh Muhammad, who reveled in such painful subjects: an Arab nobleman, visiting the Ka'ba in Mecca, overheard the wailing of a young man who had been denied his beloved. The kind and powerful nobleman took the trouble to arrange for their marriage, which was followed by a wedding trip. But on the road the bride and groom were attacked and killed by brigands. Their benefactor, saddened, planted a memorial tree to their love.

Shaykh Muhammad's first work is found in the Houghton *Shah-nama*, but his most creative flowering occurred at Mashhad, illustrating this manuscript. His enjoyment of such fierce subjects as this, along with psychologically upsetting ones (see Plates 46 and 48), marks a new, somewhat jaded ambiance at Sultan Ibrahim's court. The bloom was off the rose, due perhaps to Shah Tahmasp's ambiguous attitude toward Sultan Ibrahim, whose mood became one of "eat, drink and be merry, for tomorrow we die."

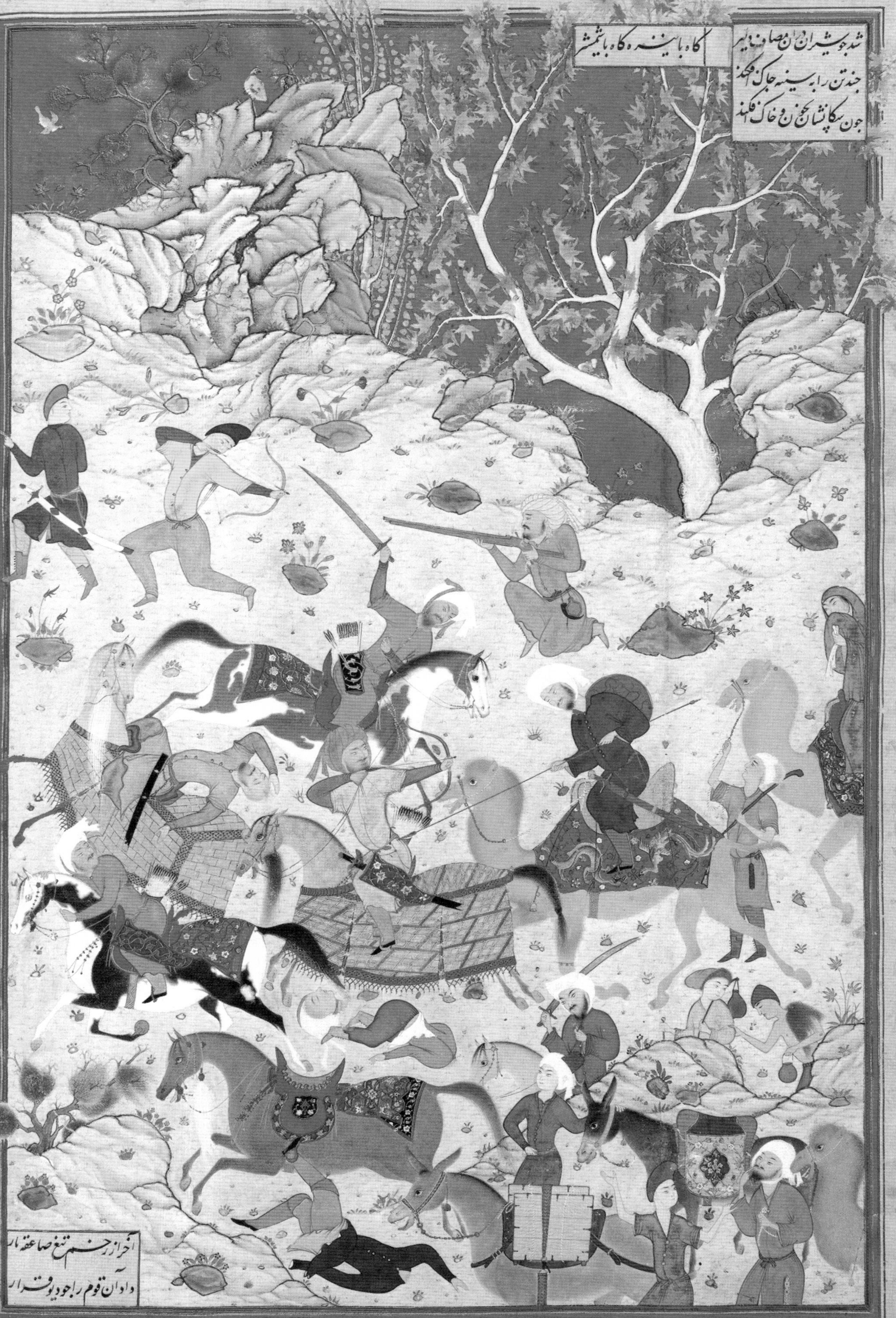
شد چو شیران در آن مصاف دلیر
گاه با نیزه گاه با شمشیر
چند تن را به سینه چاک افکند
چون سگانشان به خون و خاک افکند
آخر از زخم تیغ صاعقه بار
داد آن قوم را چو دیو قرار

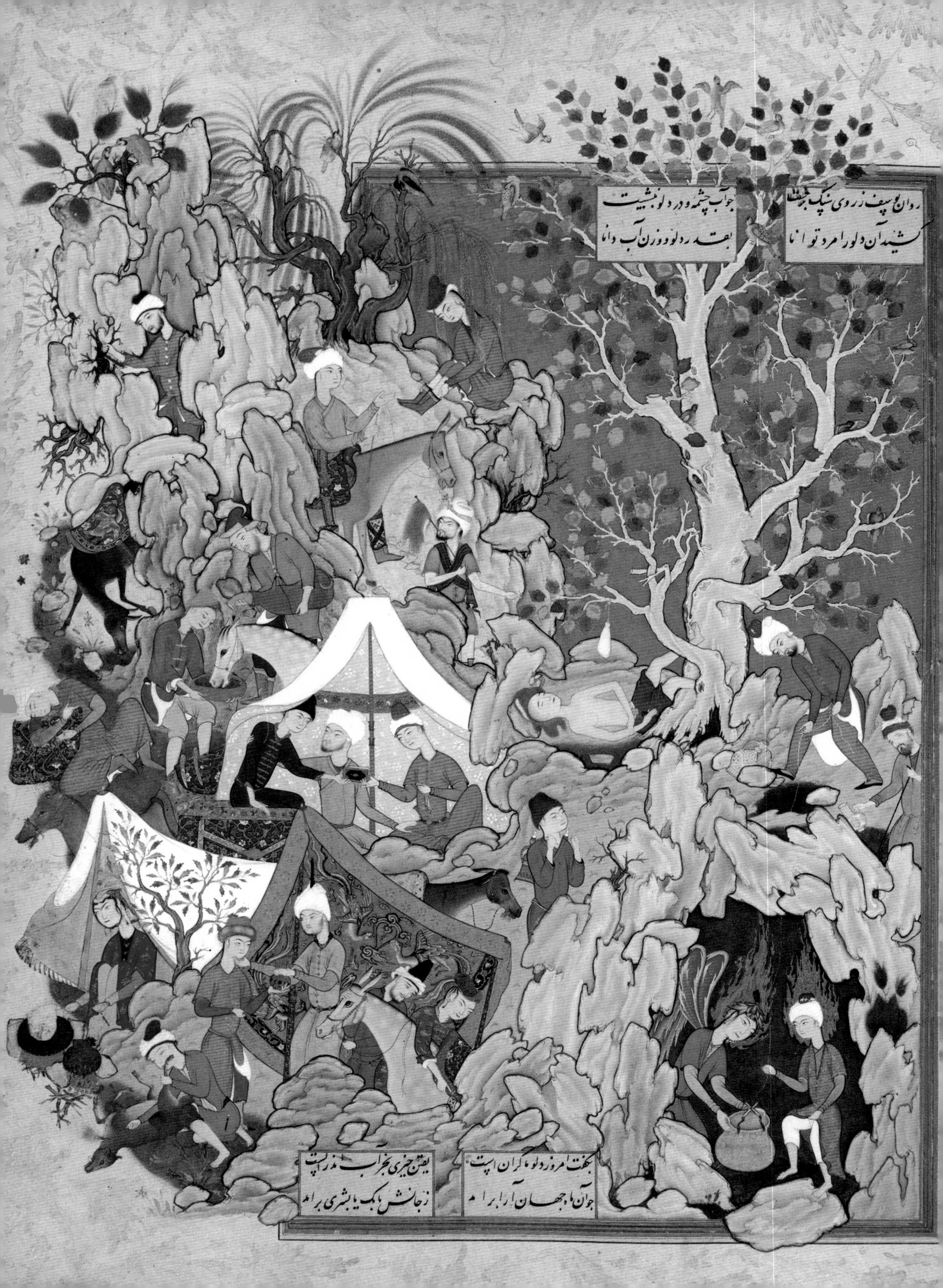
روان یوسف ز روی سنگ برجست
کشید آن دلو را مرد توانا
جو آب چشمه و در دلو بنشست
بقصد دلو و زن آب دانا
بگفت امروز دلو ما گران است
جوان ما جهان آرا برآمد
یقین چیزی بجز آب اندر است
ز جانش بانگ یا بشری برآمد

PLATE 40, folio 105 recto

Yusuf's Escape from the Well

ATTRIBUTABLE TO MUZAFFAR 'ALI

Along with stories of Layla and Majnun and Khusraw and Shirin, that of Yusuf and Zulaykha is one of the most popular in Iranian literature. Jami's version is perhaps the most mystically profound and admired. Yusuf (Joseph of the Bible) earned the bitter jealousy of his brother who tried to murder him by dumping him down a well. Luckily, the Angel Gabriel was watching over him and delivered him from it. He was then captured by slave dealers who carried him to Egypt, where his beauty caught the eye of Zulaykha (Potiphar's wife of the Bible), who bought him. The ensuing love affair was largely one-sided, as Yusuf's dedication to chastity and protection by the Angel interfered whenever she tried to seduce him.

Muzaffar 'Ali, a contemporary of Mirza 'Ali and Mir Sayyid 'Ali, placed the main subject of the miniature prominently in the foreground. The rest of the painting is an elaborate account of a courtly day in the mountains, a garden paradise well-suited to the saintly hero. Although Muzaffar 'Ali's style is very close to Mirza 'Ali's, his compositions are less architectonic, his figures less portraitlike and softer, and his brushwork, while calligraphically elegant, is less firm and fine. For other pictures by him, see Plate 45, Figures j and l.

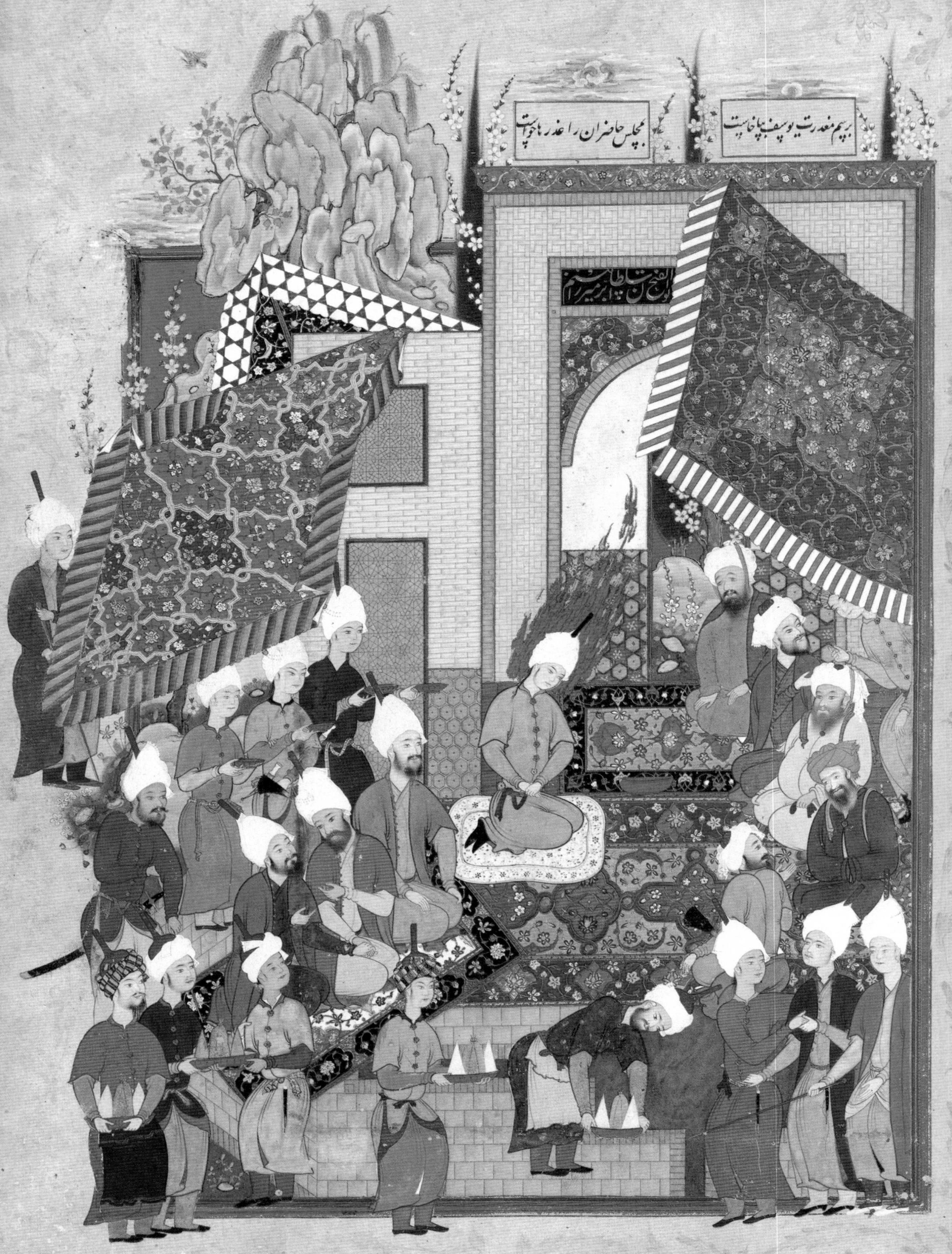

بر رسم معذرت یوسف بپا خاست
بمجلس حاضران را عذرها خواست

PLATE 41, 132 recto

Yusuf Entertained at Court before His Marriage to Zulaykha

ATTRIBUTABLE TO SHAYKH MUHAMMAD

Zulaykha's attempts to overcome the saintly Yusuf's iron-bound chastity roused her ire and led to his imprisonment, a fate from which he was delivered when he earned the Pharaoh's gratitude by interpreting a baffling dream. Before long he encountered Zulaykha, who by now had greatly aged. By miraculous means he restored her youthful beauty and when God ordered him to marry her, he agreed to do so. In this miniature the young saint is being admired and celebrated by the Egyptian Pharaoh and his court.

It was painted by Shaykh Muhammad, who flattered his patron, it seems, by rendering him as the beautiful Yusuf. The setting, with its saillike canopies and tellingly characterized courtiers, must have been based upon gatherings at the Mashhad palace of Ibrahim Mirza.

PLATE 42, folio 153 verso

Another Inadequate Gift

ATTRIBUTABLE TO MIRZA 'ALI

Determined to get to heaven, a king visited a hermit and became his disciple. Whenever he went to the holy man he brought a valuable gift, which the recipient invariably spurned. Baffled and annoyed by this, the king went hunting instead. After killing a brace of ducks, he was inspired with the happy notion that the ascetic might better appreciate these simple useful things than his previous richer offerings. But when he presented them, the holy man responded as before. At last the king understood: meaningful gifts come from lifelong devotion, the only certain road to heaven.

If we compare this miniature with the same artist's "Donkey for Sale!" (Plate 34), which was painted ca. 1556, soon after the *Haft Awrang* was begun, it is apparent that Mirza 'Ali's compositions were becoming more explosively baroque. While the earlier picture retains the taut structure associated with his miniatures for the *Khamsa* (such as Plate 26), this one breaks through its marginal rulings, like water overflowing a dam.

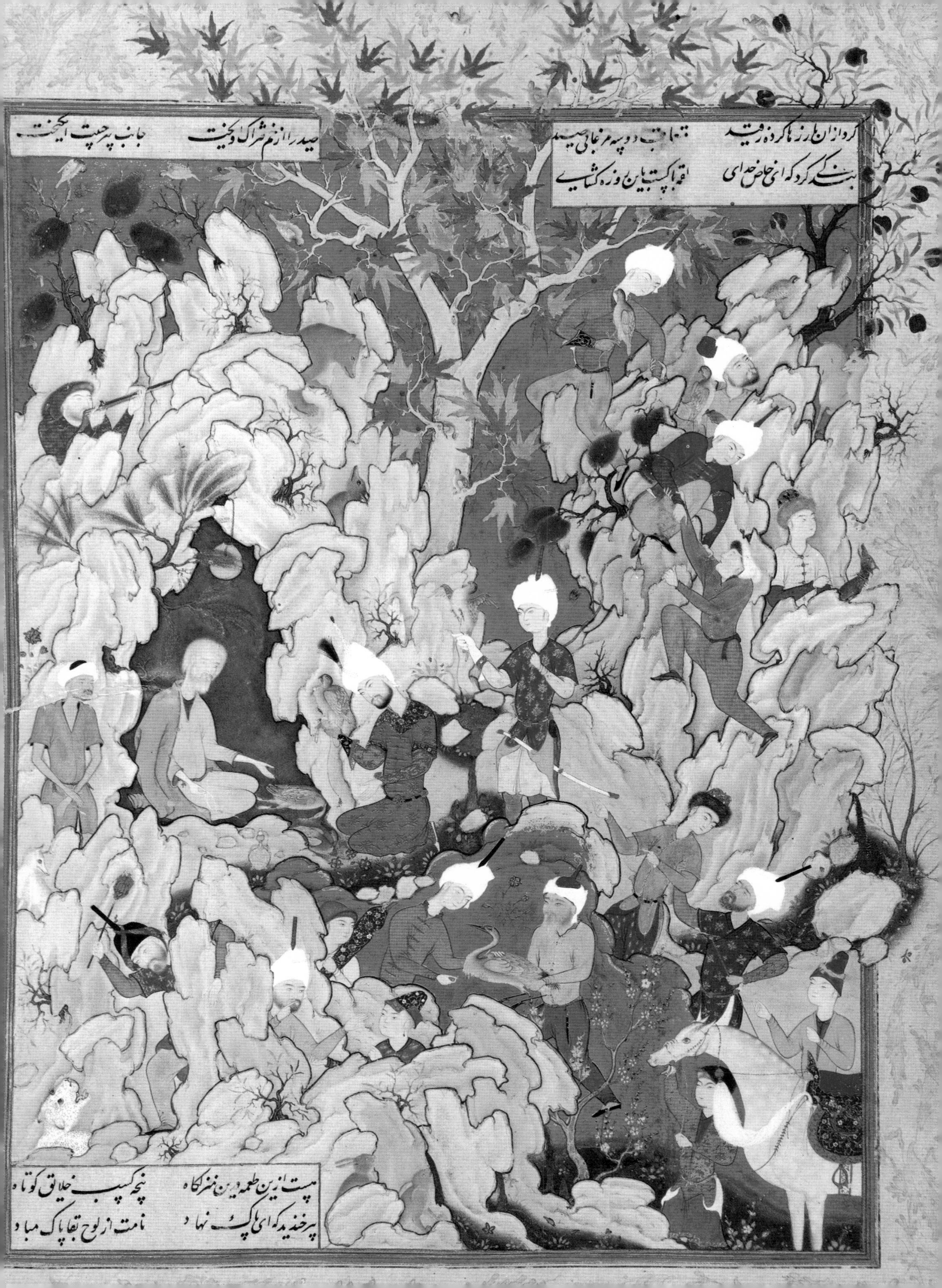
صید را از نم شراک وکیخت
جانب پیر چه حیث انگیخت
کرد ازان بارز نا کرده رقید
تیغ تاب دو سه مرغابی صید
بندگی کرد که ای خاص خدای
لقمه پاکست باین روزه کشای
هست ازین طعمه درین منزلگاه
پنجه کسب خلایق کوتاه
پیر خندید که ای پاک نهاد
نامت از لوح بقا پاک مباد

PLATE 43, folio 179 verso

A City Dweller Desecrates a Garden

ATTRIBUTABLE TO PAINTER D

To take out the knots from his heart, a city dweller wandered into the countryside. When he came upon a marvelous garden, a paradise of fruit trees and flowers, he rushed in, trampling the blossoms and boughs, and greedily plucked at the apples and pomegranates. Disturbed by this whirlwind of violence in such peaceful surroundings, the owner of the garden approached his uninvited guest. The latter turned to him and asked, "Am I doing something wrong?" "Wrong?" replied the country dweller, "You have destroyed in a moment what took years to create! How can I tell you what you have done wrong?"

The presence here of his highly personal sense of rhythm, his special profile type, and other unmistakable habits, identify this miniature as the work of Painter D, whose earliest known pictures are in the Houghton *Shah-nama* (see Plate 8).

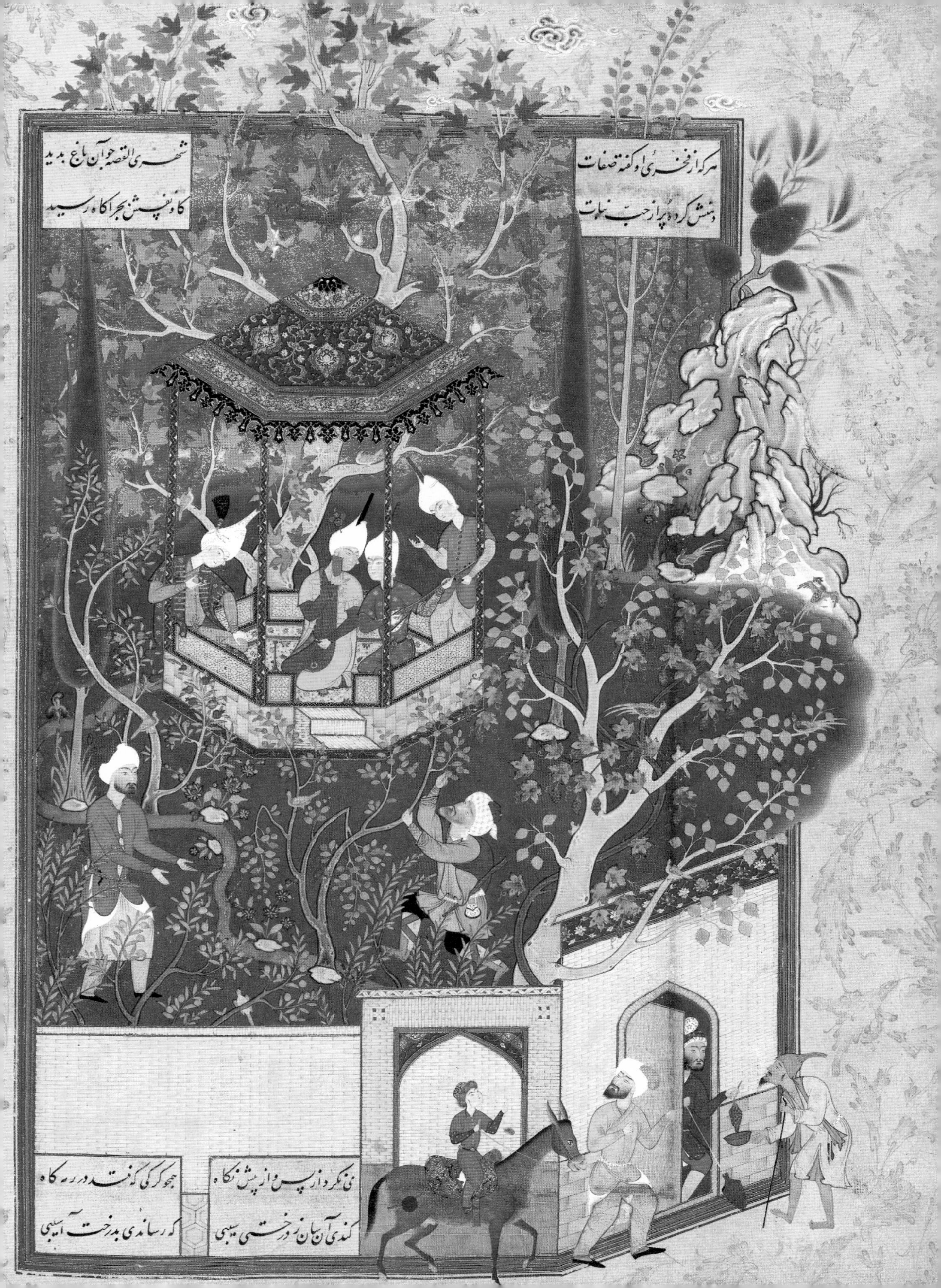
هر که از فخری او گفته صفات
دهنش کرده پر از حب نبات
شهری القصه چو آن باغ بدید
می نگرد از پس و از پیش نگاه
کندی آن سان ز درختی سیبی
همچو گرگی که فتد در ره گاه
که رساندی بدرخت آسیبی

PLATE 44, folio 191 verso

Salaman and Absal on the Heavenly Isle

ATTRIBUTABLE TO MIRZA 'ALI

The king of ancient Greece was advised by his vizier that it would be unseemly for him to have an heir by a mere woman. By magic, the vizier created an ideal young couple to produce the king's son. Fortunately (or unfortunately) the young man, Salaman, and the young woman, Absal, fell in love with one another, a circumstance that made the king wildly jealous of both. Luckily, Salaman was ingenious. To escape the royal wrath he made a boat in which they escaped to a heavenly isle.

By the 1560s, when Mirza 'Ali painted this disarming, happy picture, artists treated the human figure with increasing distortions of form. Necks became conelike; bodies were stretched to unreasonable length, with especially lean and supple chests, stomachs, and hips. Absal's figure reminds us of the flat-chested "flappers" of the 1920s.

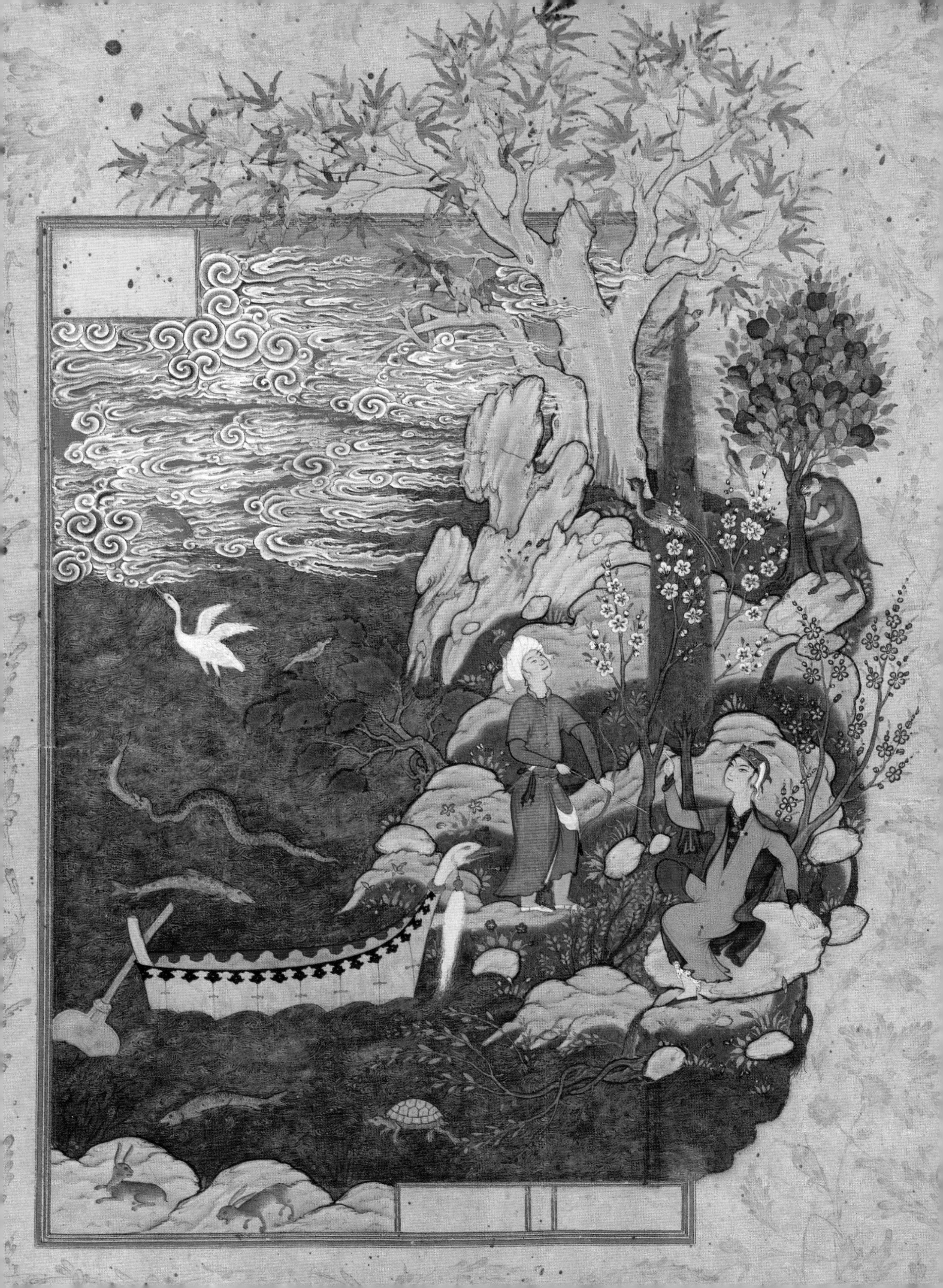

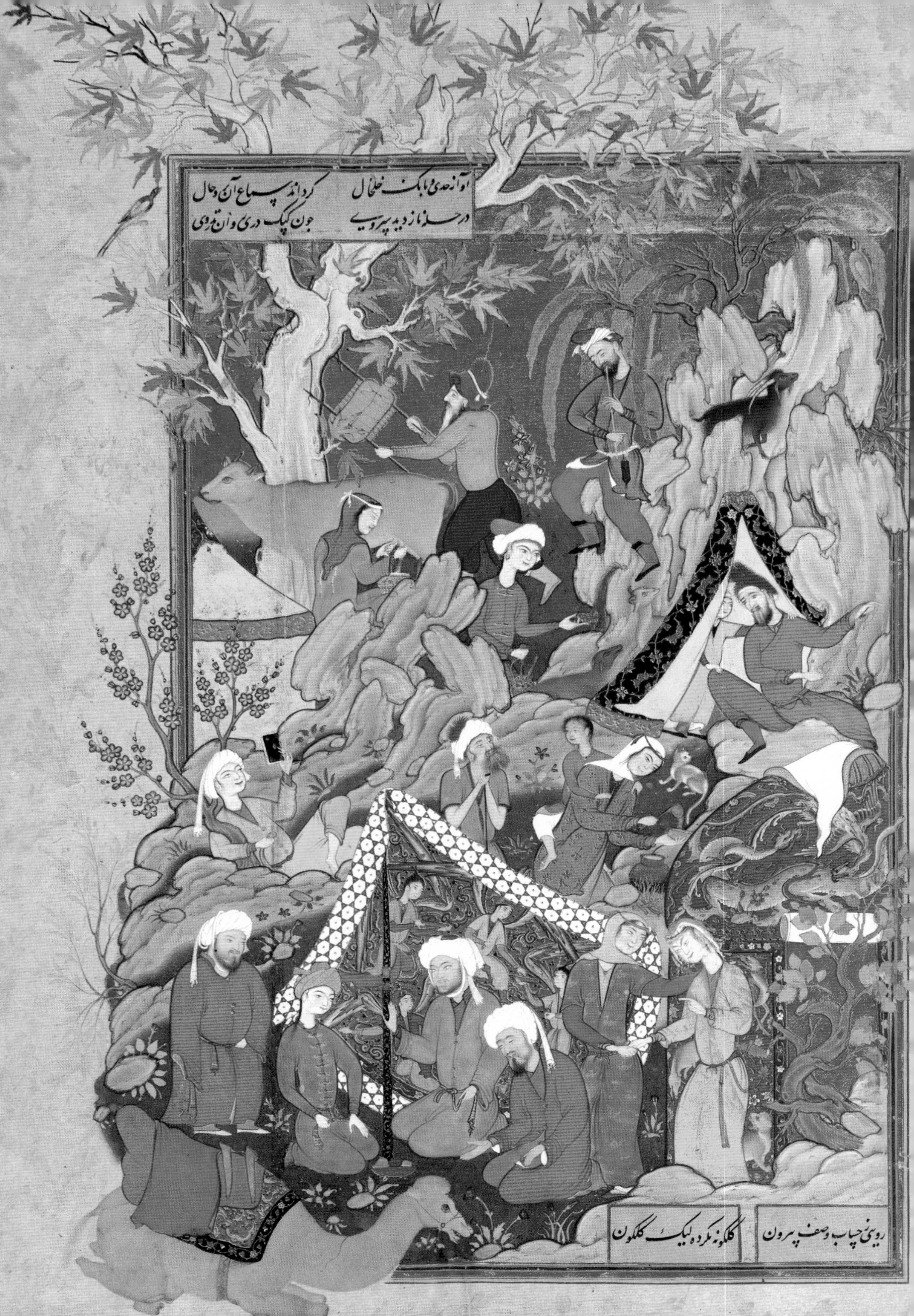

آواز حدی و بانگ خلخال
کردانده سماع آن و حال
در حله ناز دیده پیرویی
چون کبک دری و آن تذروی
روی ز حجاب وصف بیرون
گلگونه نکرده لیک گلگون

PLATE 45, folio 231 recto

Qays's First Glimpse of the Fair Layla

ATTRIBUTABLE TO MUZAFFAR 'ALI

In Jami's strongly mystical version of the story of Layla and Majnun, the boy Qays, who was later known as Majnun (see Plate 28), did not meet her in school but heard of her rare beauty and fell in love with the description. He then sought her out, and the ill-fated love affair began in earnest. Here we see his first visit to her family's encampment.

Muzaffar 'Ali's animals and dragons are among the liveliest and zaniest in Safavid painting. Coming upon an astonished, slightly angry kitten behind Layla, who emerges from her tent in the foreground, is one of the pleasures available to anyone who looks closely at this densely packed composition. Above her shoulder a mythological beast seems to echo the kitten's mood, while to her left a fantastic wolf turns out to be the cause of the kitten's alarm. But keep on looking. . . . When all the actual and ornamental birds and beasts have been discovered, still more might be found in the gnarled trees and rocks. The hunt could prove endless!

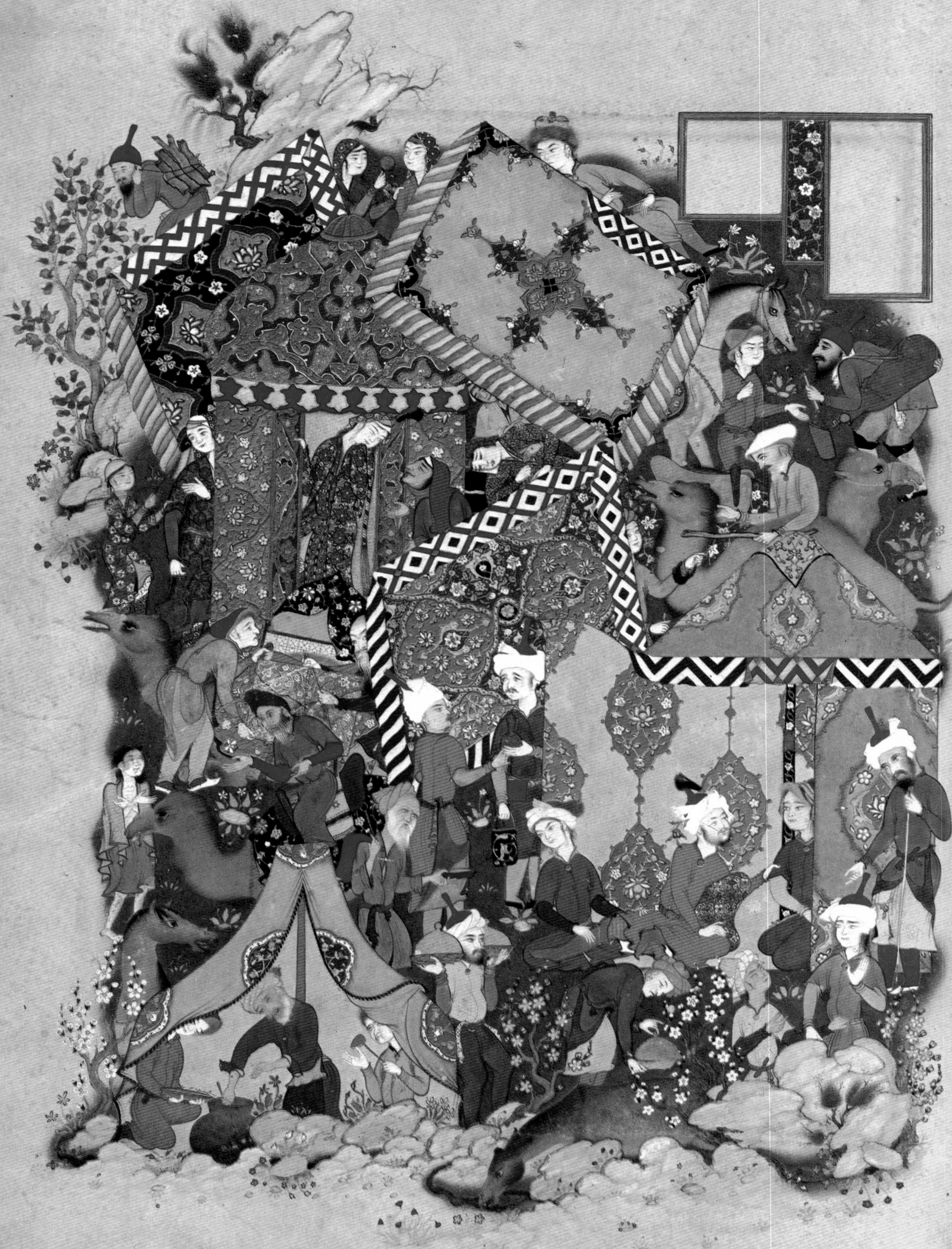

PLATE 46, folio 253 recto

Majnun Eavesdrops on Layla's Camp

ATTRIBUTABLE TO SHAYKH MUHAMMAD

Wildly in love with Layla, the daughter of his family's traditional enemies, Majnun could only see his beloved surreptitiously. In this dazzling melée of horses, camels, tents, awnings, and some of the oddest human beings in Iranian art, Majnun can be found reclining at the upper right, slyly peering at Layla who stands at the entrance to her tent.

Representative of the latest phase in the development of the *Haft Awrang*, this miniature is a far cry from the still classical spirit of the earliest miniatures. Not only have the people depicted become disturbed and eccentric, but the design and treatment of space are no longer logical or consistent.

PLATE 47, folio 253 recto

Majnun Eavesdrops on Layla's Camp/detail, *Layla pining for Majnun*

ATTRIBUTABLE TO SHAYKH MUHAMMAD

While Majnun stole into the precincts of Layla's family's encampment, she waited lovelorn for news of him.

One of the most original and inspired of Safavid artists, Shaykh Muhammad often violated the laws of "good taste." He was, however, a master craftsman who applied pigment thickly and with obvious delight. His tooling of the gaudy, burnished gold surfaces and surging arabesques make this a particularly eye-catching passage.

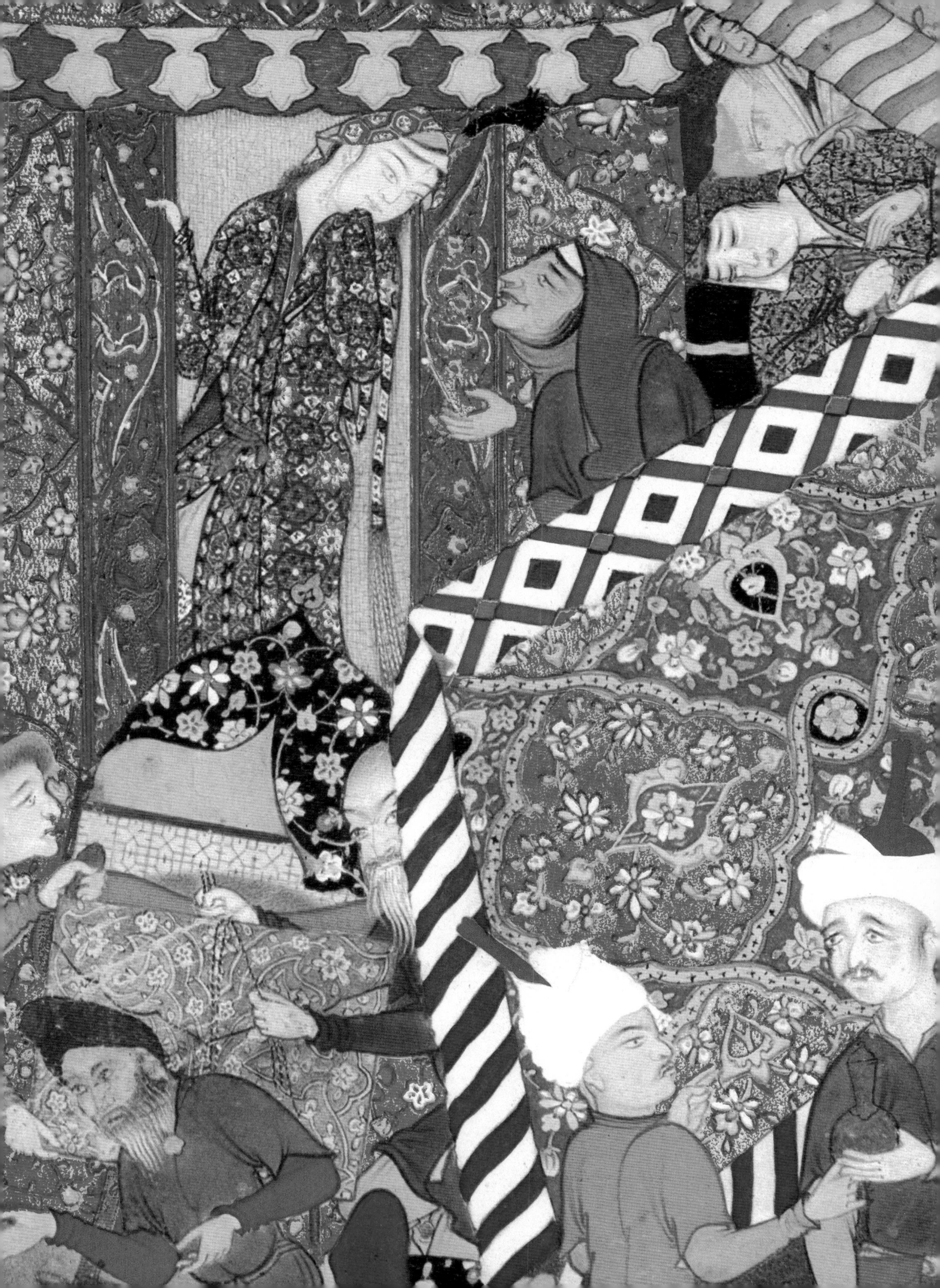

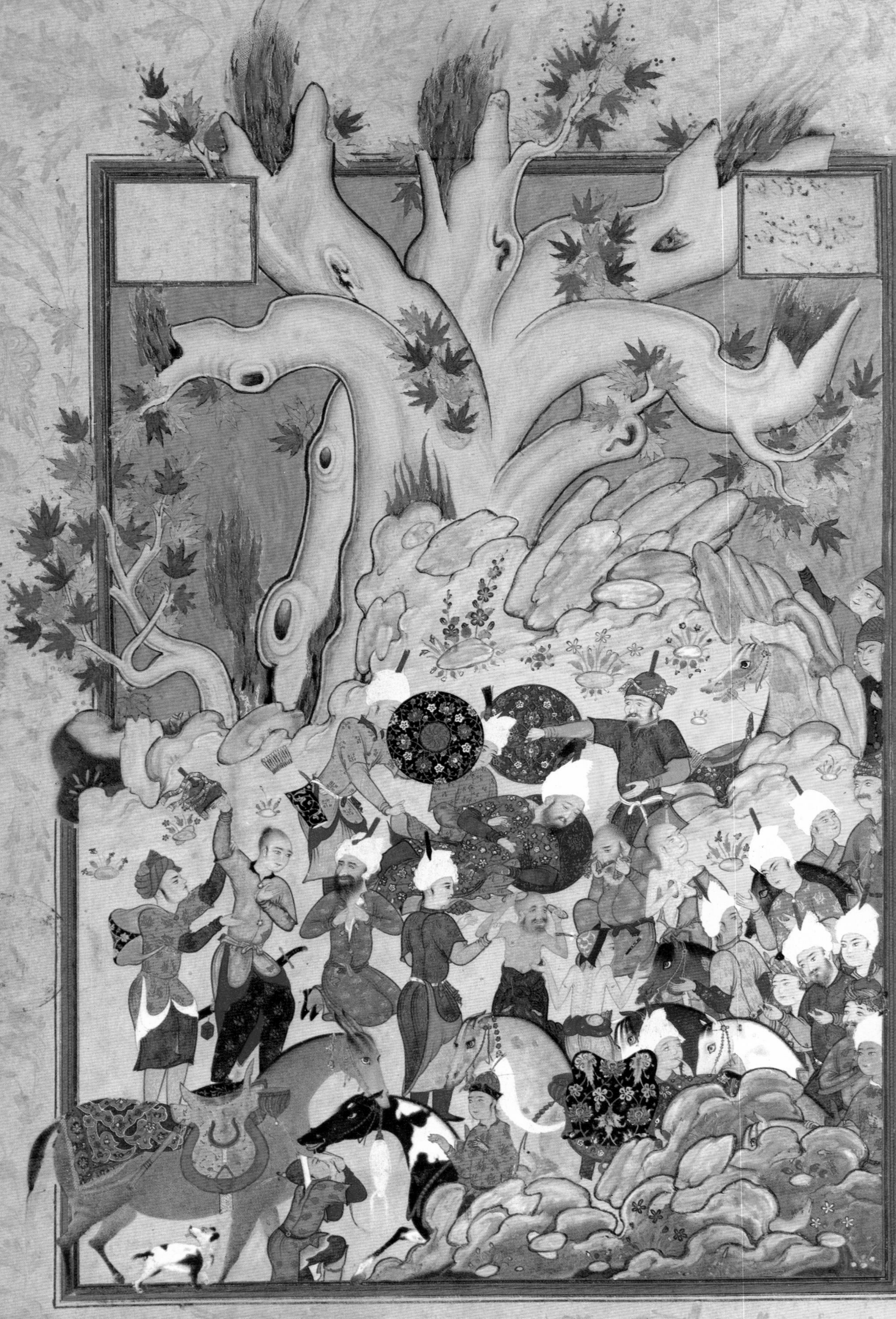

PLATE 48, folio 298 recto

Lamentation on the Death of Alexander

ATTRIBUTABLE TO SHAYKH MUHAMMAD

This is the last miniature in Sultan Ibrahim Mirza's *Haft Awrang*, which was started with delight when he was appointed governor of Mashhad in 1556. Appropriately, it ended with this illustration of the death of Alexander the Great in 1565, the year Shah Tahmasp replaced Ibrahim with one of his own sons, the very man who later, as Shah, ordered Ibrahim's execution. Shaykh Muhammad's upsetting miniature, with its vast tree, roaringly ablaze, is almost too apt under the circumstances. If the players here lament Alexander's fate, we do so for Sultan Ibrahim, and for his entourage of royal artists, who would no longer be allowed to work for him. If only they could have had the consoling satisfaction of knowing, as we do, that their manuscript was the last truly great one produced under the Safavid dynasty.